Anjan Sundaram

BAD NEWS

Anjan Sundaram is the author of *Stringer: A Reporter's Journey in the Congo* and an award-winning journalist who has reported from Central Africa and the Middle East for *The New York Times* and the Associated Press. His writing has also appeared in *Granta, Foreign Policy, Politico, Fortune, The Washington Post, The Telegraph*, the *International New York Times*, and *The Guardian*. His war correspondence from the Central African Republic won a Frontline Club Award, and his reporting on Pygmy tribes in Congo's rainforests won a Reuters journalism prize. His work has also been shortlisted for the Prix Bayeux and the Kurt Schork Memorial Fund Award. He graduated from Yale University.

www.anjansundaram.com

ALSO BY ANJAN SUNDARAM

Stringer: A Reporter's Journey in the Congo

BAD NEWS

Last Journalists in a Dictatorship

———————

ANJAN SUNDARAM

ANCHOR BOOKS

A Division of Penguin Random House LLC

New York

FIRST ANCHOR BOOKS EDITION, NOVEMBER 2016

The Library of Congress has cataloged the Doubleday edition as follows:
Sundaram, Anjan.
Bad news : last journalists in a dictatorship / by Anjan Sundaram.
pages cm
1. Journalism—Study and teaching—Rwanda.
2. Sundaram, Anjan—Travel—Rwanda.   I. Title.
PN4793.R39.S86 2015   079.675—dc23   2015005625

Anchor Books Trade Paperback ISBN: 978-1-101-87215-4
eBook ISBN: 978-0-385-53957-9

Author photograph by Freddy Bikumbi
Book design by Michael Collica

www.anchorbooks.com

Printed in the United States of America
10   9   8   7   6   5   4   3   2   1

To local journalists the world over, mostly anonymous,
who bring us information every day.

To my students.

Quos vult perdere dementat.
Those whom (a god) wishes to destroy he sends mad.

—ANONYMOUS

CONTENTS

BAD NEWS

GRENADES

I felt swallowed by the wide road, the odd car hurtling uphill, the people hissing on the sidewalk bathed in sodium-vapor orange—a tick-tock had gone off in my mind since the bomb.

And were I not so consumed by these emotions I would have savored the immense surrounding pleasantness—the long baguette-like hills on the horizon, the silhouettes of clouds that hung low over our heads, the calm city that offered so much space—that tonight made me feel disoriented, smothered.

I searched for charred metal, the smell of burning rubber, any remains of the violence. A blue-uniformed policeman stood near the traffic circle, tall and rigid. I raised a hand to signal him, and spoke almost in a whisper: "*Mwiriwe!* Good evening! Was it here, the explosion?"

"The what?"

"The blast. I heard it from down the hill."

"No, no, you are imagining things." He spoke slowly, shaking his head.

"What is that man sweeping, though?"

"We always clean the roads."

But I saw fragments shimmer, and I made to take out my camera.

His hand moved in front of my face. "No photos! *No photos!*"

"What's the problem, if there was no explosion?"

"Listen carefully. Nothing happened here." I instinctively stepped back.

Everybody in the neighborhood had heard it. I was told the ambulances had come—their sirens silent. But the road was now practically clean. Traffic was circulating, as it always did in Kigali, in orderly fashion. And the center of town, in this, the most densely populated country in mainland Africa, was nearly empty, as usual.

The discussion in my classroom two days later only heightened the sense of insecurity. Ten journalists arrived, and one by one took chairs. The mood was somber. The curtains fluttered at the back of the room. A stout young man said the blast had been caused by a grenade, thrown to destabilize the government.

The journalist had succeeded in taking photographs, but the police had recognized him and searched his bag. They had found the camera and taken the film—many journalists in my class still used old, outdated equipment—and warned him to wait for the official version of events, not to promote the enemy.

There was a murmur of discontent. The faces in the room were all marked—some by hunger, by fatigue, others with deep gashes. I heard a wooden knock pass the classroom door—it was the figure of Moses, hunched over his cane, stumbling over a leg that had been smashed in a torture chamber.

Moses, a senior journalist, had been responsible for summoning the students to our training program. He was so respected that not a single person had refused his invitation.

The students were newspapermen and -women, both owners of publications and employees. Most were in their thirties, though some were much older than I was. They had been specially chosen for our training program for their independence and ability—the idea was to bring together and professionalize

Rwanda's last free journalists, so they functioned as a skilled unit.

I had come to Rwanda to teach journalists how to identify, research and write news stories in this program. I had spent the last two years in America, but prior to that had worked in neighboring Democratic Republic of Congo as a journalist for American news outlets. I was familiar with the sensitivities of news in this region, with its history of conflict, and was eager to return. I wanted to help these students be successful journalists.

Our program was funded by the United Kingdom and the European Union. The mandate was to help these journalists report mostly on government initiatives, such as efforts to make people wash their hands or see the doctor. So the program had been approved by the Rwandan government. It had existed for ten years already. But now it had become a place where these last journalists could work together.

The grenade in the city had come as a reminder of violence. It could have been thrown by armed dissidents. It could also have been an act of the government itself. Regardless, the regime would use it as justification for a new round of repression.

"I don't know if we can survive it this time," a student said.

"The government is making arrests. Secret prisons."

"Many developed countries were once dictatorships. Tell us how they obtained their freedom."

The stout young man said the last time he was beaten he had been blinded by his own blood gushing over his face. It was because he had mentioned the harassment of journalists at a press conference, in front of the president. His name was Jean-Bosco, and he ran a popular newspaper. He had been left in a coma for four days after that attack.

"But we have to keep speaking out," a female student said.

"That's our only defense. The more we speak the more the government will be afraid to hurt us, along with the other activists. And we have to stay together, no matter what."

The speaker was a short young woman with a red bow in her hair. She had just spent a year in prison after criticizing the government. She was sick with HIV, and had endured psychological and physical abuse while in prison. The prison officials had screamed in her face until she was tired, dragging her from room to room so she could not rest. Her name was Agnès.

The room had turned quiet.

Someone muttered: "How can we fight a violent state. Is there a way out for us?"

"America gives them weapons. Israel trains their secret service."

It happened that we were approaching the twentieth anniversary of the fall of the Berlin Wall, and there was a series of commemorative writings about that period.

I read them one such article I had recently come upon. It was a reflection by a former Czech dissident, about his struggles to create a political opposition, and about how everyone had thought him ridiculous, his task impossible, until the dictatorship suddenly crumbled.

Agnès stared at the other journalists.

The Czech dissident spoke about his efforts to create news pamphlets and underground information networks—it was a battle with the dictatorship, a battle to keep alive the information that the regime destroyed, suppressed.

And I felt it was important that he described his pamphlets: for the journalists in that class were from the newspapers. The written word, in a dictatorship, offered possibilities that the radio, often used by dictators for propaganda, could not. The written word offered subversive possibilities in a dictatorship, offered some hope of freedom.

It has been so in every revolution, even in the Arab Spring, in today's digital age. Writers are often at the forefront of revolutions. And it often is they who bear the brunt of the repression.

A radio broadcast requires equipment—an emitter, an antenna. The speaker on the radio might be recognized, and killed. The equipment can be destroyed, leaving the revolution mute.

But the written word belongs to no one. It has no source, no root that can be annihilated. It passes from hand to hand. It is destroyed; new words are written.

And now more people have begun to write, there are more sources. The written word can thus become something sacred to a people seeking freedom, to a revolution.

I collected the homework from the previous week—a report about a city hospital—said goodbye to the students, pulled the white cotton curtains over the windows of the classroom hall and began the walk to my house.

Moses hobbled beside me. It was another peaceful, cool evening. I felt the exhaustion of the day of teaching. I didn't mind his slowness. A sympathetic taxi driver, Claude, saw us on the road and offered a lift. Moses, grateful, climbed into the beaten-up car.

At home, I poured myself a cup of tea and arranged a seat on the balcony. From here I looked over a large garden, and farther down into a green valley. This was without doubt the most beautiful city I had lived in.

The house belonged to the training program. It was commodious—four bedrooms—and had once been a diplomat's residence. Unaccustomed to so much space, I occupied only the common areas and a bedroom whose door, the landlord had eagerly pointed out, was bulletproof.

I went through the homework. And there was a surprise. I had come to know my students well—but a certain Gibson, a quiet man in his thirties who always sat at the back of the room, had written a remarkable report. The ideas were organized logically, almost without error. He was not afraid to ask large questions. And the hospital was vivid in one's mind: its doctors, the children.

Feeling slightly buoyed, I made for my bedroom. Briefly I turned on the radio. Still nothing about the explosion from the other night. No acknowledgment that it had happened; no sense that people in the country had been wounded or killed.

I did not have to wait long for the pressure to take effect on the journalists. The first notion I had was during a series of pronouncements by the president, Paul Kagame. I expected he would at some point address the explosion, which had been a surprise, even incredible. Rwanda had known an extraordinary calm over the last decade, a calm nearly as absolute as its genocide sixteen years before had been violent.

The president spoke slowly, his voice shrill, almost like a bird's. He spoke about democracy in the country and the freedom that his people enjoyed, and how sad the coup d'états on the continent were, being the result of the absence of democracy. These were at his political meetings, press conferences, ceremonies in football stadiums and at the opening of a new factory. He was a tall, emaciated man, whose suit billowed over his body. He seemed innocuous, laughing at his own witticisms. But he could make or condemn people, villages and entire regions with words—it was almost as if his spoken word became reality, became the world. His was the voice of the nation; this was possible in the dictatorship, for mere speech to attain such power over living and dead things. So when he spoke there was great silence. His words were broadcast all over the country, with the regularity of a drumbeat; and on the windy hilltops and in homes, the people strained to listen.

The president had fled these same hills as a child. He was only three years old when, in 1960, an uprising against the Rwandan elite forced his family to flee to Ugandan refugee camps. So he began among the dispossessed. As a young man he fought with a Ugandan rebellion, becoming that country's head of military intelligence and receiving training in America. In 1990, he commanded a force of Rwandans who had broken off from the Ugandan army and invaded Rwanda. The invasion set off a protracted conflict that the president called a war of "liberation" and culminated in Rwanda's 1994 genocide. The end of the genocide, in July 1994, was like a new birth for the president, as he took power in Rwanda.

Kagame's control was at first something that needed to be divined. He was the vice president, the minister of defense. Others made the speeches and the state visits. But over time Kagame had done away with his front men. He had Rwanda's previous president arrested for five years, and then pardoned and released him without explanation. The radios now broadcast Kagame's slow speeches.

Some were permitted to ask questions at his events. "Your Excellency, why are so many countries eager to study our roads, hospitals and poverty-reduction programs? Is it because the country is developing so rapidly after the genocide?"

"Our country has learned a lot from its history," the president said. He added that he was happy to share what had worked for Rwanda, and what had not, with anyone who was willing to learn.

The radio crackled, radiated these ideas of the authorities' success. "Your Excellency, I was asking myself the other day why our government is so capable and professional, why we have so little corruption. Our business ratings are so good. The World Bank, the United Nations, the Americans and the British are praising us. But what is the cause for the praise? Yesterday I realized the answer. It is our leadership, Your Excellency. This is our secret."

I recognized that last voice. It was Cato, one of my students. I felt something piercing in my stomach. He had decided to turn, and evidently join the president's army of flatterers— a group officially called the Intore in Rwanda. By praising the president they incited fear and devotion in others. It was the easiest way to protect himself. Our class had lost a student, but I did not blame Cato; the situation was too precarious for all the journalists.

I found a frightened Gibson in his apartment. He asked me to close the door at once. "Have a seat." His sofa was a wooden frame with soft square cushions, all covered in an old bedspread's maroon cotton. Besides a small center table this sofa was the only piece of furniture in the living room. The apartment had whitewashed walls and was lit by a dim lamp. It had a single bedroom. Gibson lived in a shantytown on a slope of an eroded mud hill.

"I bought the sofa just a few days ago," he said. "Do you like it?"

He was clearly proud of this somewhat pathetic acquisition. I said I would find him some new cloth. He became immensely pleased.

I had come with an idea to travel with Gibson. We were entering the season of memorials for the genocide, in which some eight hundred thousand people had been killed over a hundred days—a rate of murder unequaled even by the Nazis—and in great pain, for they were killed mostly with machetes, not guns.

It had been an idea of mine since I had arrived in Rwanda, to pay homage to and remember those who had died from this human cruelty. But Gibson furiously shook his head. He said it would be too dangerous.

He was a man sized like a fourteen-year-old boy whose hands trembled lightly when he reached out to pick up things. Perhaps to hide this, he wore shirts with sleeves too long that extended beyond his wrists and up to his hands. The shirts were often white and hung over his small shoulders. And besides his best friend, his former roommate at the seminary, he was something of a loner, rarely mixing with the other journalists, who teased him for eating his *fou-fou,* a paste of manioc flour, with his fingers, in a way that tried to imitate the manner of city folk—it immediately gave him away as someone who came from the countryside.

And here as well, in his apartment, he was ashamed of his poverty. I could see it in the way he passed hurriedly into his room. He had little to offer though he had known I would come. A large bottle—shaped like a canister of liquid detergent—containing diluted and sugary apple juice was brought out.

He poured himself a glass but did not drink it.

I asked what he thought might happen if he traveled with me.

He shrugged, seeming to search for words.

I congratulated him on his hospital story, which had won a prize in our class. There had been visible consternation from the other students, particularly Jean-Bosco—no doubt from a sense that Gibson was a peasant boy, and did not have the requisite dissident credentials. Gibson had himself been surprised, and had stood stunned, looking at his certificate during the prize ceremony.

I suggested he try to get his story published.

He shook his head, smiling. "My newspaper will never publish it."

"There's nothing political about your piece," I said, insisting that his editors would not turn down a well-written story.

But Gibson had for some months been writing for the country's main independent paper, *Umuseso,* The Early Morning. It was Rwanda's most popular publication, revered by the people. Within hours of a new *Umuseso* edition vendors had to sell photocopies—such was the demand. Even in far-flung villages, where few could read, one would find old copies making the rounds, being read aloud by the literate. The print press was sought after in Rwanda, as few had access to the Internet.

The government had begun to crack down on *Umuseso* reporters, many of whom had once been close to the president, even living in exile with him. Some *Umuseso* journalists had already fled the country; others were in hiding. An old court case had been resurrected and the lead journalists found guilty of defaming one of the president's powerful accomplices. The president hated criticism.

But like a many-headed hydra *Umuseso* survived the government attacks. This was not an ordinary newspaper. Its stories rarely cited sources, and were rarely verified. Yet they were often accurate. With astonishing success *Umuseso* predicted which officials would be fired or accused of corruption or sexual misconduct. The paper's source was the regime itself. There were officials deep within the government, who publicly supported the president but who felt certain information should be known, and had for this reason become leakers.

This made *Umuseso* the most important paper in the country—its journalism was the only kind that had any meaning in the dictatorship. And the people had long ago learned that it was in presidential office gossip, rather than the theatrical parliamentary or ministerial hearings, that they should look for clues to their future.

The association with *Umuseso* meant Gibson led an extraordinarily private life. He used a neighborhood boy to fetch him beer in order to avoid being seen. And when he got out of the house he quickly escaped, he said, to a distant neighborhood where there was less risk of being recognized.

I turned down his offer of a drink, and asked how often he saw his family.

"Sometimes I worry for them. But it is better we don't see one another. My work could endanger their lives. It is better like this." He sounded as though he was trying to convince himself.

He mentioned that he had a girlfriend. "I would like to marry her. But who would marry me? I have no money, and I am always worrying about the government. I can't offer a girl much. I would like to have a child and raise a family. Sometimes I wonder what it would be like to have a normal life."

He looked around the room.

"Have you read Hegel?" His eyes sparkled.

It had been a while.

"I think his concept of the dialectic can help describe my life. Two ideas are opposed, and they give rise to a greater truth. Sometimes I feel this is why I confront the authorities."

He added: "I think it is also because I realized many years ago that God was dead."

Gibson often cited one of his mentors at the seminary, a bishop who had edited a newspaper. This bishop had written against the poor prison conditions and the harassment of human rights workers. The authorities had seen him as a threat. When the bishop fell ill, the government prevented him from traveling abroad to seek medical treatment. He subsequently died.

We then exchanged some philosophical banter, though I was unable to keep up with him.

"You don't know how much this conversation means to me," Gibson said. "I am always closing myself in, and my mind loses sharpness. My professors, friends, I have given them all up. I don't have anyone to talk to except poor people. I have nothing against them, I am a modest man, but this kind of exchange of ideas, I have not had it for a long time, and it makes me feel somehow alive."

He read to me from a recent edition of *Umuseso*, which he had salvaged from a government raid on his former apartment—the authorities had been looking for traces of the leakers within the regime. In this *Umuseso* issue was a story about how the president's chief of cabinet had contrived to remove her predecessor, who had fled to Belgium claiming he would attend a training program but had never returned. When the government was silent about those who had fled the people were scared to evoke them. Outside of the independent newspapers it could seem as though these exiles had never existed.

There was a knock on the door.

Gibson froze. Fortunately it was he who had been reading, and I had been silent.

The knocking repeated.

I sensed his terror at being seen with me, and I slipped into his bedroom. Here in this poor neighborhood, not frequented by foreigners, there would be suspicion about my presence, and what we were discussing in private. In his bedroom the floor was covered with stacks of handwritten papers. I moved closer; they were notes for a news report.

Gibson spoke from the doorway. There was a tense discussion between him and a man—it seemed a census of some sort. After a while I heard the door being shut. I waited some moments.

It had been the Intore, the group that Cato had joined. The presidential election was coming up and gangs in the neighborhood were going house to house to ask, "Are you sure you know whom to vote for?" They were also holding a celebration in the president's honor, and forcing people to attend.

Gibson was sweating.

I asked if he would go. We spoke more quietly now, pausing often, our ears alert for even a slight movement outside.

"Sometimes I tell them that I am sick, and hope they go away. But you can't avoid these events for too long. They are the duties of a 'good citizen.' I too have to go and chant for the president. It is necessary if you want to eat."

I took my leave. Gibson, seeming disappointed, picked up my empty glass, and said he normally would have walked me back.

Before leaving I asked about the explosion. Any news? The event seemed to have almost passed into my imagination. Gibson said there had still been nothing.

Closing the door on me, quickly, he seemed deep in thought. I sensed a despair had grown within him over the evening. As I walked out a small exterior light came on, to help me navigate the uneven mud, shaped with crevices by running water. I looked up: the moon was ringed by a glowing halo. It would rain tonight. The light was put out as soon as I stepped out of range—I turned, but could not spot from where he was observing me.

I slowly made my way down the red hill, tripping, my mind occupied.

A helicopter moved over the city, shining a powerful spotlight on the neighborhood around me—it was the police's night patrols.

I thought much about Gibson in the days that followed: I admired the man. In his tranquil brown eyes, despite the fear, I sensed an ambition and defiance. He seemed sure of his resistance and in his quiet way courageous. I suppose it moved me that he did not come from a wealthy family that could afford dissent: no. I felt I should do everything to help him, even if it occasionally involved risks.

Gibson was still writing for *Umuseso,* but only "harmless" stories. It was not the moment to be provocative, he said. The genocide memorials seemed to make the journalists newly nervous. In the classroom, again I asked why he would not visit them—I thought Gibson could write a simple story about genocide survivors. He shrugged. I grew frustrated at his evasiveness.

I arrived late to class one day. At home, I had turned on the national television—the country's only channel, it was what people watched when they wished to see the president delivering a speech, or documentaries on topics they were permitted to talk about: the country's mountain gorillas, development projects, criminals captured by the security forces. I saw images of people hacking at one another with machetes.

It took me a moment to understand what I was looking at. And then I felt a new, visceral kind of terror. It was a bloody, insane slaughter.

I watched a grainy video of a roadblock on a red dirt road. An unarmed figure—a man? a woman?—was assaulted. A machete came down on the figure, arcing high through the air. The figure fell to the ground. The machete came down harder and harder. Now the camera moved close up, showing bodies on the ground, on the grass, in latrines. The blood over them was thick black. A piece of a head was missing. Another body was sliced open at the stomach so one could almost see its internal organs. Children, women, men.

Everything about the genocide terrified: the sheer number—eight hundred thousand—of dead; that thousands of ordinary people had participated in such a vile act; that it had all occurred in only one hundred days, between April and July 1994; that so few had seen it coming; that when presented with proof the world had turned a blind eye and done nothing.

On April 6, 1994, the official airplane carrying the then Rwandan president, Juvenal Habyarimana, was shot down, killing him. The genocide began shortly after, as did a military advance by Kagame's forces, which had invaded Rwanda four years earlier. The country at that time was facing an economic crisis, and was ruled by what used to be the farmer class—the Hutus. Kagame represented a section of Tutsis, the traditional Rwandan elite, who had been exiled just before Rwanda gained independence from Belgium in 1962. His invasion stirred fear that the Tutsis would continue an old history of subjugation, and radio broadcasts during the genocide goaded the killers to exterminate Tutsis so the people of Rwanda would never again be oppressed.

The victims suffered alone. As the killings in Rwanda mounted, and the evidence of genocide became clear, the United Nations voted to decrease its troop numbers. The United States shied away from recognizing the atrocity as genocide for fear that it would be compelled to stop the killings.

The national television channel showed us more bloated bodies beside a river, and then a church that had become a mass grave.

Kagame achieved his military victory during the genocide, taking charge of Rwanda and imposing order and calm. His government now regulated minute aspects of the country's functioning.

The journalists I taught and the ones at independent newspapers like *Umuseso* were both Hutu and Tutsi. Some were from the families of Tutsi genocide survivors, others from the families of Hutu killers now in prison.

That day in class, during the tea break between lessons, I asked Gibson about the images broadcast on national television. He silently picked at his piece of sponge cake. We were standing outside on the classroom porch. Gibson seemed too distressed to tell me much. I felt the broadcasts had touched a nerve, and that he was trying to shelter himself from such emotions when he refused to accompany me to the memorials. I knew he had been a boy in Rwanda when the killings had occurred. He smiled and mumbled something about the season of memorials. And I sensed it was more than the history that terrified Gibson, for his fear seemed rooted in the present, in how the genocide was now felt. I needed to seek counsel, for I did not fully understand.

I spent the afternoon teaching the class how to construct the lead paragraph of a news story. The paragraph needed to contain the essential information and grab the reader, yet be brief. We attempted some examples together: the students and I started with the same story, about a flood in America, and each tried to write the best lead.

Then we received news that the government was going to shut down *Umuseso* and also the newspaper run by Jean-Bosco, the student who had once been beaten into a coma. Jean-Bosco had not come to class that day. Several students did not believe the reports. "That would be going too far," Gibson said, particularly of *Umuseso*. "We are supported by powerful people, close to the president himself." He was sure that come Monday new issues would be published and available on the streets.

I called Jean-Bosco. He confirmed the government pressure, but said he was fighting it from every angle and that his paper would soon be up and running. That night I made another round of calls to my students, to learn if they had more news, and also to see if they were all right.

But less than a week later we learned that Jean-Bosco had been alerted that his life was again in danger. Government agents had followed him and told him to make a "U-turn," to stop his reporting and help the government or they would "finish" him. He had fled. It was rumored that Jean-Bosco had crossed the eastern border, over the river, into Tanzania, perhaps as a way to get to friends in Uganda, and that the security services were working frantically to capture him.

The repression did nothing to help Gibson's nerves. He stopped talking much on the phone for fear that we were being listened to.

And the country was still imperturbably quiet, calm. A visitor would have no notion that any of this was happening. No one demonstrated or spoke out. Radios and newspapers continually relayed good news about the government, besides information about the ongoing genocide memorials, and briefly mentioned the criminal journalists.

I passed a difficult few nights.

It was Moses, the elder statesman of the journalists, who showed me the extent of the threat that was looming. The repression was having wider, transformative impact. I told him about my discussions with Gibson. He shook his head, and said there was an acute risk as the journalists were gradually silenced: the changes in the country, he said, were irreversible. Matters had become critical and needed to be written about. "You are concerned for the lives of the journalists. We must look after them. But how can they be idle now? The government is doing things that need to be stopped, and it is destroying our ability to have any kind of discussion."

He was grave about the recent events, particularly I thought for a man who was so respected by the other students—it made me alert. "You have to understand, in all this," he said, leaning over his cane, "that there are not many journalists left."

I had come to his home to collect him. Moses was escorting me to a memorial.

We were to go to the place where the genocide took root in Rwanda. It was in the north of the country—it was there that the president's forces, then in rebellion, had begun to attack the previous government, launching incursions from the mountains. And it was here that the previous government had conducted retaliatory killings, rounding up and killing everyone of the rebels' ethnicity—already, at this early stage, thousands of people.

I got to know Moses personally at this time. I learnt that he was in fact a survivor of the genocide. During the hundred days of killing he had hidden himself in bushes while street boys had fed him bread and wine that they had stolen from churches. Moses had reported on the genocide by the previous regime at risk to his life. Now he had committed himself to working against the repression, though more discreetly because he was older. We boarded the bus that would take us north. Moses told me he would like to write about some of the president's crimes.

I asked why he wasn't afraid of speaking to me, in the open, at such a tense time, when the other journalists were being so cautious. I was thinking of our program, and also of Gibson.

His answer surprised me. "I died during the genocide," he said. "My entire family was massacred. I should have been killed with them. Now what's there to fear; are they going to kill me a second time?"

He called himself one of the walking dead. It seemed many survivors of the genocide described themselves as such.

Did he go often to the memorials? Not in a long time, he said.

He had attended them in the beginning, just after the genocide. Indeed he had created one of the first committees to organize remembrances. But soon the government had taken over the memorials.

This was our conversation, to the sounds of the pop music that played in the bus, as we traveled alongside the beautifully forested hills, to the town of the memorial.

Moses had gotten me on a special bus normally reserved for survivors of the genocide and their families. I spent the first hours listening to the chatter. And I would have remained silent—I had begun the journey in a sacred spirit, thinking of the dead—if there was not a general lack of sobriety in the bus. It was the Western pop music, and the laughter of the passengers.

I tried to pry out of Moses what he wanted to show me. He was crisp: "You'll see."

He added: "You know, to control people you need to create a great deal of fear."

I asked if there was much rancor against the president for the people he had killed.

I was referring to crimes committed during the genocide and afterward in Congo. The president's forces had killed tens or perhaps hundreds of thousands of people. His army had invaded Congo, sparking a war there that still runs today and has killed many millions more, mostly from hunger and disease. The president had said he was hunting down the perpetrators of the genocide in Congo, but his forces reached nearly a thousand miles into that country and installed a new government there while slaughtering unarmed women and children en route. The massacres in Congo had been documented in U.N. reports—which had called them acts of a possible counter-genocide—but the killings in Rwanda were still shrouded in mystery. The president had suppressed investigations. When I asked Rwandans about these deaths they said, "I know nothing about them."

Moses and I started to talk without mentioning names so people would not know we were referring to the president.

"He's killed a lot of people," Moses said, "who will never receive justice. Many Rwandan families cannot name their dead because he was responsible." Moses waited a moment. "But did you know he also killed his fighters, including his child soldiers? It was a policy in his rebel forces. There was a word for it, *kufaniya*. It means 'do something for him.' That kind of ruthlessness, we started to realize it later. He cares for nobody. Even his wife means nothing to him. I think he is a little sick in the mind."

I asked why a man would kill his own people.

"He only knows to rule by fear."

Moses had become perturbed. "He grew up as a refugee. He returned from exile with his army and conquered this country. A Pygmy senator, after that war, said that when the big man and his people left Rwanda they had to leave their stomachs at the border, and go with their nobility, so people abroad would care for and feed them. But when they returned, they found these stomachs at the border, hungry for thirty years. They left behind their nobility, and picked up the stomachs."

I waited. Moses became bolder and now mentioned the president.

"Nobility is very important for our people. Politeness, generosity. The president kills people who fought by his side, who protected his life, and were like his brothers. Where is the nobility in that?"

We had nearly arrived—the hills had grown larger and larger, and were often capped by forests. It gave the idea of a natural countryside. But on closer observation one saw that the thickets of trees on those hills were made up of a single species.

They were plantations of eucalyptus, brought in by the Belgians during the colonial time. So there was little natural about the countryside.

And the undulating land, which at first seemed lush, one saw was everywhere divided into rectangular patches—each a shade of green, yellow or brown, depending on the crop. Here, unlike in Kigali, it was possible to sense how populated the country was, occupied to every inch.

The music, as we arrived, changed to religious tunes; the volume was raised. In the bus there was a general fidgeting; a sense of purpose had come over the passengers. Feeling it was inappropriate to talk I leaned back in my seat. Moses was looking out of the open window, his hands holding the vibrating glass. At the venue I saw a van with a satellite dish broadcasting the event across the country.

We walked into a battery of wails. Several thousands of people huddled on a field, dressed in purple, the official color of the memorials, and hurling cries. Women rolled on the ground; others fell over the men beside them. Immediately it began to rain—the sharp cold rain of Rwanda, accompanied by an enveloping mist. We pushed ahead, Moses with his cane, among the incessant cries of increasing volume, and arrived in the center of the field at a set of white stairs.

At the top of the stairs was a white platform, on which stood a man screaming into a microphone: "Repent! Repent!" Music began alongside the wailing, repeating the words: "*Jenoside, Jenoside.*"

I climbed the steps. A group of poor-looking people were lined up behind the speaker, and they had begun to cry. The women began to beat their breasts with palms and fists. And they pushed forward their children—five and seven years old, bawling, with snot dripping from their noses and over their tattered shirts.

I felt a tugging on my shirt. It was Moses. "You see what he is doing?"

There was a pleading look in his eyes. Leaning over his cane, he was totally concentrated on my face.

Coffins began to be carried below the staircase, into a white crypt. The coffins had glass tops, so one could see inside. In the first were skulls, neatly arranged, one beside the other, clean and perfectly shaped. I could not help but fix on one of the skulls, and imagine its past: the anger, hatred, fear, desperation. In the next coffin were femurs, set along its length. A dozen boxes passed by. "Repent!"

This was strange, for the culture of Rwanda would value preserving the dead body as a whole. Even if only a femur and a fragment of bone had been found after the genocide, they should be buried together, to represent the body, honor the dead. But the victims had here been dismantled, and their bones regrouped by part; it had the effect of emphasizing the number.

The children were now crying so hard that they had to stop to gasp for breath. Their voices were strained, grating. They coughed, and liquid spilled out of their mouths. Why had they begun to howl, and bray? *"Jenoside! Jenoside!"* These children were too young to have been alive during the genocide. But they behaved as if they possessed its memory.

And one realized that the memorials also served the purpose of transmission. And that the transmission was meant to cause distress. It was as in Rwandan schools, where teachers complained that during the memorial season the videos on national television made the children uncontrollable. But despite the teachers' complaints, the gruesome films continued. I was doubly horrified: I had expected something else from the memorials: some compassion for society, but I felt only violence. The government of Rwanda had created these events, which instead of healing society, increased its trauma. The terror of the genocide was being used and spread. One realized that the genocide and the time of war, almost two decades past, were still kept alive in the country. The trauma of the genocide was, in the children, running like roots through society.

"They are manufacturing fear in these places," Moses said, gasping. "We survivors have asked them to stop this violence. What do they want from us?" I could see he had begun to shake, that he had lost strength in his legs. "Sometimes I cry to myself at night. Like this"—he put his teeth over his lips and started to bawl—"not because of the memories of the genocide. But because of how the government mocks the genocide, uses it to get pity from the world, to get money, and at the same time keep us in a state of fear."

The crying around us was alarming.

"The imbeciles, the imbeciles," Moses repeated. He seemed not to care about the government officers standing nearby. "The imbeciles who run this country are negating us, using us, selling us. They are building our country on our bodies, our blood. They hold shows like this, theaters, and pretend. This place is the trauma. They put people in prison for negating the genocide. But if they were serious about it then the first man in prison would be the one who ordered this."

Moses said there were other places: military-style camps across the country for children. Kept far from society, the children spent weeks in them, were dressed in military fatigues, and indoctrinated to be utterly devoted to the government.

The president each year held an event, at which he brought thousands together in the national stadium: films of the killings were played, the crowd was driven into a traumatized frenzy. And the president reminded everyone that he was their savior.

There were other places as well.

"We can't say anything," he said. "And when the president is done, no one will want to."

On the journey home it took Moses several hours to regain some sense of calm. "I don't know if we will succeed against this," he said. "But God knows we have to try."

The explosion had by now become something vague in the mind: the memory of its sound had receded, and the shimmering swept-up glass had acquired an unearthly glow. Without acknowledgment, or any proof, evidence, without the shock that society should normally feel, without a sense of an emotional response from the country, I began to wonder if the explosion had happened at all, if it had not been something I had imagined. It was frightening, that something so obvious to the senses as an explosion—that had wounded and killed— could turn into a sort of hallucination, and be made to disappear.

LIGHTS

In the classroom Gibson suddenly said that he wanted to start a magazine. It would not flatter the president, nor print overtly subversive news. He wanted this magazine to fall somewhere in the middle of the spectrum of newspapers in the country, and hoped it would one day publish his hospital story.

The anger was lurking; the news was harsh. Already among the journalists only the uncompromising still dared operate. "The more they harass the press," Gibson said, "the more aggressive the news gets, and the angrier the government becomes. Perhaps we can break this negative cycle with some sense."

But he looked away from me as he spoke. I suspected that the stress had become overwhelming. He saw few ways to report honestly without drawing the authorities' wrath. Gibson was trying not to react to the government's pressure on him, to remain calm as the tension mounted. That week he had stopped writing for *Umuseso*.

He asked what I thought. I told him I wanted to help. Gibson said his best friend would join in our efforts.

He would call the magazine: *NEW HORIZONS*.

What Moses had foretold began to be. I continued to teach my journalism classes. Without Cato, who had turned to the Intore, and Jean-Bosco, who was being pursued by the government, it wasn't the same. I invited new journalists to take their places, so we still had ten students. But the classes were quieter.

Discussions were less vibrant. It took longer to get through basic material.

Gibson still sat at the back of the room. Agnès was there as well, scowling as always, her back to a wall. I was glad for their presence. Sometimes I felt I was teaching mostly for them.

A student brought in a copy of a government paper. It was in Kinyarwanda, the local language. A picture of the president was on the front page. I asked the student to read out the first paragraph of the lead story.

"Victoire Ingabire, the criminal with genocidal ideology, will be prosecuted by the government . . ."

She was an opposition politician who had been living in the Netherlands, and had returned to run in the upcoming election against the president. One of her first acts in Rwanda was to visit a genocide memorial and say that there were many others who had been killed but were not remembered—she was also referring to those massacred by the president's forces, all mention of whom was suppressed.

I looked around the room at my students. My cup of tea from the morning break between lessons was growing cold.

I asked if there was a problem with the news story. No one answered; this alone was unusual. Before, it would have been difficult to contain the students.

I asked them if the politician, Victoire, had been tried in court.

After a pause, some of the students meekly shook their heads. They sat on either side of a long conference table, at whose head I stood. I scribbled from time to time on a flip board. Now I wrote: "Court."

"No, she has not been tried, and is therefore not a criminal—not yet," I said.

"But the president has said she is a criminal," someone countered vociferously.

"Does that make her a criminal?"

It was futile, for the courts depended entirely on the president. Reformist judges had been expelled so the president controlled the judiciary. This was how dictators destroyed countries, to gain power: they destroyed the capacity for independent speech, then independent institutions—and ultimately independent thought itself. I was bearing witness to this process of destruction, and trying to reverse it.

"Who wrote that story?" I asked. It was the newspaper's editor in chief. "Is he experienced?"

When no one else volunteered Agnès answered that he was indeed experienced, that he had been a reporter for twenty years, and had on many occasions written good, balanced stories. There had been fierce competition for his job.

I reiterated my point: "Is he incompetent? Or does he know what he's doing?"

They murmured, though before they had been reluctant: "He knows what he is doing."

"Then why does he write like this?"

Silence again.

A student finally spoke up: "He wants to make the president happy. The editor in chief knows what he is doing is wrong. But to please the president he will not only agree with what the president has said, but go even further. Out of an excess of zeal. He will accuse Victoire, indict her and judge her for other crimes. It is how we are taught to show loyalty—"

"One journalist has written that Victoire had extramarital affairs. It has no relation to her case. But the government likes to smear its enemies. So we do the job for them, even without them asking."

"When you flatter the president you receive favors, promotions, money."

A woman interjected: "How do you expect otherwise? If we

don't call her a criminal then the authorities think we are on her side. They have even threatened my children. But if we say she is guilty they leave us alone. So we even call her a villain, genocidal . . ."

A free discussion had begun, at least. It had taken some work, but with the assistance of the original group of students, the other journalists were now expressing themselves, debating, thinking, supporting each other, helping one another speak.

I knew that I could not hope to fight the system on my own. But I wanted the classes to be a catalyst, to create a feeling of solidarity, so the journalists knew that they were not alone— the regime was trying to isolate them, and pick them off one by one.

And I could see that the students already knew the answers— even if these were buried deep within. They needed courage, and the solidarity of their colleagues, to speak their minds.

"This excess of zeal is a problem," Gibson said. "We say things we don't believe, just to please some people, and we end up believing what we say."

"To stop flattery we have to stop being afraid."

"It makes us forget the truth."

I had given the students assignments—to visit schools, clinics, agriculture programs. Their stories had more errors than when I'd had the more experienced journalists. I spent hours outside the classroom making corrections.

But the work felt rewarding. Every day that I drew the students out of the repression I was satisfied. I felt that a small part of truth had been won that day. And there seemed hope that this piece of truth could grow, and live.

The office, where I taught the classes, thus became a place of great energy, a place that gave me strength. Class after class was conducted; the students advanced, developed camaraderie, and became more adept in their reporting. With limited resources and funds, I felt our training program was making a real difference in the country.

Gibson would stay on in the office in the evenings, and together with his best friend, the former seminary roommate, who was to lead the business development—Gibson would be chief editor—we drafted a detailed business plan. The government required this for the magazine's registration. One had to show enough funds for computers, tables and chairs; an office, the government said, had also to *look* like an office. The regulations were meant to dissuade journalists, and make our work difficult. We joked amongst ourselves that the government would soon also mandate the color of journalists' socks. I offered Gibson the use of our office facilities, which had ample chairs and spare computers when the other students were not around.

It was a fulfilling period, of long hours of work with good spirit, during which our friendship grew stronger and more complete.

I understood Gibson better as the magazine took shape, and became increasingly convinced of his sincerity, his courage and intelligence. We grew excited by the possibilities the magazine offered. The project began to occupy our minds. We felt that it would almost certainly succeed with the public, and might even turn a small profit in its first months, if we were lucky.

I remember the office garden from this time. Our office was blessed with an enormous garden that had a quality of privacy and splendor. I had been told that before the genocide it used to be a favorite sitting place on Sundays for the former president's daughter. It had a large scaly guava tree with spreading branches. We could see this tree from the rooms in which we worked, and I associated its scattered form with many strong memories. I was delighted to have gotten to know Gibson.

A first copy of the magazine was printed. The front page was in color, and he had even found a couple of advertisements, which were of simple design but impeccably printed. It was an admirable effort.

The design, the copy, the printing, the advertisements: all this had been achieved with little fuss. Gibson worked in silence, on his own, as if unaware of his intelligence and his progression. He was lost in his work. There was never the disturbance of achievement.

He still kept his distance from the others, spoke to no one, had no real friends besides his former roommate.

The main story in this first issue was about malnutrition. The government position was that Rwanda had sufficient food and that the president's policies had banished hunger. Gibson had avoided confronting the official line. Without ever stating that Rwanda had a malnutrition problem, and that children even in the capital—the beacon of the government's message of its success to the world—were dying from the condition, Gibson simply provided information to mothers that would help them feed their children.

Fundamental needs of the population like food, housing and health were especially sensitive topics. They were essential to the discourse that the government was doing good for its people. The government might point out problems that arose, but for a citizen to do the same, to say without prior signal for example that people were lacking food, was inherently dangerous. It was seen as diminishing the government's authority. Even posing the question could be seen as a form of displeasure, dissent. It was why one always added that the government was doing everything necessary. Or to be safe, one avoided stating the problem at all.

Language was thus made complex. It was as much for your use as for use against you. The attempt to write or say something, to express yourself, turned into an intricate exercise. Distrust or unhappiness might show in a word, a pause, a twitch. One had always to feel that one was being watched. And that anyone could use what you wrote or said—or what you did not—to denounce you.

What then was the truth about how people were faring? The president was declaring to the world that he was creating progress: he was growing the country's economy, reducing poverty, reducing hunger. But he suppressed verification of these claims. For instance, when the World Food Programme announced a famine outbreak in Rwanda in 2006, affecting hundreds of thousands of people, the government denied it. To this day, there was officially no famine. When the United Nations released a study in 2007, signed off on by Rwanda's finance minister, saying the number of impoverished people in the country had risen, and that hunger would remain above levels in 1990—the year the president had invaded Rwanda to "liberate" the people from the previous regime—the government forced the United Nations to discredit its findings and blacklist the researchers. A World Bank research team studying the country's progress, directly testing the president's claim that he had improved life in Rwanda since 1990, was forced to destroy the data it had collected when it became clear that the study was willing to contradict the official narrative. Subsequent research teams, at the government's invitation, have found that the economy is growing, poverty is declining, and that people are better nourished. Researchers investigating police corruption were expelled from the country; the country was declared among the least corrupt. A magical nation was thus created.

The government's telling of history was rich in such deceptions. An irony of the memorials was their slogan, "Never Forget," which to many Rwandans, even genocide survivors, meant the opposite. Rwandans had to forget, for example, that the president had opposed the deployment of U.N. peacekeepers one month into the hundred-day genocide. The president had worried that the peacekeepers would interfere with his military campaign, and prevent him from taking power. Thousands of deaths in the genocide could have been avoided, besides the scores of civilians his forces had killed. But the president had cast himself as the hero of the genocide, as the man who had ended it while the world stood idle.

There were some outlets, like my students' newspapers, where people still dared to describe their lives and memories. Otherwise, one could not question the government's statements, so what the government said became the truth.

Gibson had realized that the solution was to write around these official narratives. In this way he would address the immediate concerns of the people, but ensure his own protection.

One afternoon Gibson came to the office with news we had been waiting for. The ministries of information and health had both approved *New Horizons*. We had been optimistic about approval since his publication was not critical of the authorities. It was a good sign. Gibson's pimpled, cratered face showed both satisfaction and a kind of melancholy. He would soon be able to publish.

Gibson had already charted out the next four issues, their themes. He had lined up journalists, and spent his own money, from the little he had saved up, to pay them for their reporting.

We went to the garden that evening with some bottles of beer. They were almost the size of wine bottles, the standard in Rwanda. Once Gibson had made sure no one could observe us he drank his beer through a straw. It was the traditional way. In villages men would sit in a circle and pass around a flask of banana beer—a practice the government had outlawed. I think Gibson quietly enjoyed his small subversion.

One still felt the nervousness in the country. The *Umuseso* journalists had been summoned to court. Their lawyers had asked the judge if the president had sent in a complaint, perhaps a letter, as proof of his irritation with their newspaper. The prosecution asked if that were the only way to know of the president's irritation. So this landmark case, with serious implications for the country, would devolve into a discussion about the president's possible emotional states.

"Maybe *New Horizons* will become a way for journalists to open up spaces to speak," Gibson told me. "We can get the message out while worrying less about the government attacking us. People in our country are dying needlessly. If we tell them how to cure themselves they will survive. We just have to be patient, and help a few of them at a time."

The garden had grown more and more splendid. We were in the rainy season, and the humid afternoons came with sharp, heavy showers. The clouds would then quickly disperse, and the sun would light up every blade of grass, every leaf, flower.

In the twilight hour Gibson and I observed the birds with long orange tails, the African paradise flycatchers, swoop down from the guava tree and pick out the flies that hung in midair as though in a stupor.

Gibson was now considering a point of business: should he publish the magazine as a stand-alone or would it be better to distribute it as a supplement with existing newspapers? He felt the latter would be more feasible, particularly to begin with: he would avoid having to build a distribution network, and wouldn't have to craft a brand from scratch. I had not seen any paper use such an idea in Rwanda. I observed the young man. He looked nonchalant, and unaware of his ingenuity.

We heard a noise above. A helicopter plunged toward the city. Gibson and I stepped back. It was not the night police— the rotors were set higher and the engine had a more powerful, smoother sound. It flew low, almost recklessly low over the houses. A professional pilot on his own accord would not fly in this manner. The machine, its belly slender and white, hovered to one side of us. The chops became hard, suddenly audible. I wanted to hide. Feeling exposed, we shielded our eyes, and tried to get a view of the person in the cockpit.

There was a high wall, at the top of which hung a small square picture of the president. And in front of me, against this wall, was a scrawny man wearing a thin T-shirt and khaki shorts. The man smiled repeatedly at me. We stood outside a conference room.

He looked up, at the photograph. And then at me.

I looked up as well. And at him.

He started to laugh. It was a cackling laugh, hysterical and high-pitched.

I laughed.

"It's funny, no?" he said.

"You're funny."

He was unfazed. "When he's watching you, you know everything's going to be all right."

I smiled at the man.

"Careful, careful, he's always watching."

"Only small eyes here," I said, looking up.

"Sometimes the photos are big, bigger even than the man."

He asked if I had been to a certain hotel. I had not.

"Got a photo so big they have to put it on a chair, next to the receptionist. No space on the wall."

A pause. "They had problems with the man, you see," he said, raising an eyebrow. "A big photo pays for your sins."

I smiled at him again, and turned in to the conference room. It was in one of the city's best hotels. The government was holding a seminar on political reforms—I had not been invited, but I stood near the entrance.

A number of foreign human rights organizations had recently criticized the government. Some reports had been released—about the "increasing threats, attacks and harassment" and "serious incidents of intimidation"—that had presented the government in an unsavory light.

The authorities, in usual fashion, had first said that there were no such problems in Rwanda, then that it wasn't the business of foreigners how it ran the country. But the president cared about his image abroad. The government organized a conference on the questions, promising to enact reforms if problems were indeed found. Senior government officials were mandated to oversee the effort.

The major embassies had been invited: from the United States, the United Kingdom, the Netherlands and Sweden. The European Union, the World Bank and the United Nations had sent their officials. They sat in a row at the back of the hall and observed attentively.

Two Rwandan journalists in the audience stood up and spoke against laws that criminalized reporters for minor offenses. Another said that government officials never returned his calls. No one mentioned the harassment by the police and secret services; it would have been too dangerous.

The government officials, sitting on a stage, looked these journalists up and down. One of them nodded at the speakers, closing his eyes from time to time to acknowledge what they said.

This official promised that the issues would be addressed. Committees would be formed. The journalists would be represented by a man the government trusted—a former police officer had been named to head the Rwanda Journalists Association. It was a way of hijacking the journalists as a group: anyone wishing to hear the journalists' point of view would be presented with this former policeman who adhered to government doctrine.

People would be able to speak freely, the government man assured the audience, glancing to the back of the hall.

Refreshments were offered. I managed to grab a samosa and some passion-fruit juice from the platters, and watched the Rwandan journalists, some of whom ate as though it was their only meal of the day.

As I passed some of the British, American and Swedish embassy officials on my way out, I asked what they thought. They said they would closely watch the government's actions, and that of course human rights had to be respected.

I came out with mixed feelings, but harboring some hope. With the foreign governments watching the president might be forced to improve conditions. Perhaps my journalists and their work might still have a chance.

From the small photograph the president seemed to look down on us benevolently.

I didn't see the scrawny man in the khaki shorts approach— I was exiting the hotel, walking beside the embassy SUVs rumbling out, when he arrived with such speed that I was stopped in my tracks. He introduced himself: "My name is Roger." The smile was still intense, penetrating. He said we needed to talk. Not now and here, he said, let's do a meeting. We exchanged numbers—he gave me his scribbled on a paper scrap, and said I should give him a call.

"Of course," I said, but then completely forgot this man, as a number of things happened too quickly in the two weeks that followed.

The magazine was having difficulties. It had received approval from all the relevant authorities—even the one for economic development. And the first issue of *New Horizons,* of which Gibson had printed a small sample run, was receiving exceptional praise. Strangers were writing in by SMS to say that they adored the articles and were already using the information. We were on the cusp of the launch. But a government media regulator—reporting directly to the president—blocked the publication.

Gibson was never told that he was being refused registration, but each time he went to this regulator they requested a new form, a new certificate from some government arm, a new letter stating his intentions. It began a cycle of debilitating, and Kafkaesque, confrontations with officials. Gibson was made to repeat information he had already given them, but in different form, on new sheets of paper; he was made to provide irrelevant information; he had to obtain testimony from the authorities in his home village that he had been on "good behavior," that he had attended the community work sessions, had not been outside at irregular hours and had not received odd visitors. That the man had no criminal record did not matter, of course—the people close to the president needed to ascertain that he was not associated with any rumors of suspicious activity.

How to defend himself against rumor? The threat was formless. In a dictatorship it wasn't the facts that determined one's life, it was the claims, the whispers, feelings. There was no escape from the cloud of rumor following, invisible. Still Gibson ran from authority to authority, trying to please officials, trying to provide every proof that they asked for. He was beside himself, fatigued, overcome with worry that his project would be crushed.

And one afternoon his former roommate arrived in the office while Gibson and I were working. The friend was trembling. He sat down. He had been called that morning to the parking lot of a nearby hotel. The callers had said they were from a ministry dealing with one of the authorizations. But when he arrived he found plainclothesmen carrying revolvers—government men—who snatched his telephone and scrolled down to see whom he had been calling. The men said they wanted to talk to Gibson. The roommate told us he had said his friend was traveling, that he did not know where. And after the interrogation he had run first to a gas station, to make sure he was not being followed, and then come to the office.

He had taken a great risk by coming here. Someone might have seen him.

Gibson was immediately tense. He let forth a flurry of questions—Why him? Did the men say what he had done? He had written nothing overly critical, he said—nothing, in any case, compared to the other *Umuseso* journalists. He could only think of his reports in *Umuseso* about government trials to prosecute killers from the genocide. Gibson had mentioned suspects close to the authorities who had not been charged. But he had written these many months before, and his recent reporting had been benign, as were his plans for *New Horizons*. Was even his malnutrition story now unacceptable? He became quiet and told me at the office, once his friend had left, that this was not normal. "I am very worried."

The friend and he had agreed that they should no longer talk or meet. Gibson had to move out of his apartment at once. But where could he go?

The editor of *Umuseso* had just fled Rwanda. The threat had become too pronounced: the government had begun a widespread witch hunt in the country for journalists from the newspaper. So Gibson was not alone in his danger. But these journalists each faced the government individually; they were already isolated.

We did not talk about what would happen to *New Horizons,* and Gibson said he was trying not to panic. The journalist had a plan. It was out of the question to stay in the capital after what had happened, so he would leave for a little while. Perhaps the tension would die down; perhaps the government had something personal against the *Umuseso* editor; perhaps the government would find a distraction and leave Gibson alone. He would hide himself and watch from a distance. He didn't even tell me where he was going.

He suggested it so naturally that I thought it must have been a plan he had formulated long ago, in case of such a situation. And the next day he was gone.

I did not think he would travel near his family's home; that would not be intelligent. I wondered if Gibson would be safe.

He was pitting himself against a system that was incredibly powerful. It was the same system that could eradicate its explosions. The state was highly ordered and controlled. Every piece of the country was organized into administrative units benignly called "villages." Each village, or *umudugudu,* contained about one hundred families. Even the capital was but an agglomeration of such villages. The president called his office Urugwiro village. Each village had its head, its security officer and its "journalist" or informer, all of whom had to approve of one's behavior if one wanted something from the government— a passport, for example. The system's power was shown in seemingly innocuous happenings: slippers were worn overnight by masses of villagers following a government order. Plastic bags were suddenly eradicated from the corners of the country. To achieve such control the government had relocated thousands of people in the countryside to new "villages." Directives from the government now could be followed down to the individual. And there was no privacy. Officials and security agents in the villages kept track of visitors and those traveling. Permission was required if someone was to stay overnight. Hotels every day sent records to the security services, with the names of visitors, using Rwanda's network of well-paved roads. Where was Gibson going to hide?

I asked Moses if Gibson had been correct to flee. I also asked if he might protect Gibson for some time, and shelter him, should he return to the capital.

Moses said he could house the journalist for one night. Beyond that it would be too dangerous. In fact, if Gibson was still in the country he could not afford to stay more than a night in any place.

He said that people everywhere wanted to please the state, and would go out of their way to report the outsider who had come to their area, particularly if the arrival was suspicious. The whole country was, in effect, watching Gibson.

It was how the people participated in the country's control. There was a powerful contract between the government and citizens. The state, extending through the people, became omnipresent. In other dictatorships dissidents were able to move between cities, wear disguises and change identities. Anonymity gave them the possibility of freedom. Rwanda's *umudugudu* system made this impossible.

Moses said, "If Gibson is really being pursued by the government, and he is still in Rwanda, there is a good chance that he will disappear." Such a benign word, *disappear,* for an event so brutal.

I imagined him on the run, from city to city, hotel to hotel. He called occasionally, never for more than a few minutes, and often just to tell me he was all right. I think it reassured him to talk to me, as he ran without destination. He knew that the government could use his friends or family—he needed to escape his former life and everything he knew. It was thus a kind of illusion, trying to run away. Though he was courageous to try.

And after two weeks of gradually closing in, the government finally caught up. Gibson called me to relate how it had happened. There was a knock on his hotel room door one night.

He asked who it was.

We had always believed that it would be the secret service or the police who would come for him. But no, the government had used someone who knew him well.

"Your friend, James."

I felt let down: James was another of my students. He too had won a prize alongside Gibson. He was a government radio employee, known for his independence, and had spoken passionately in the classroom in favor of freedom. I had held some hope for him. And now I felt slightly broken. Perhaps he had been offered a promotion, or a loan to build a house. Though rewards were often unnecessary—it was reward enough to be seen by the government as loyal. I had lost two journalists at once.

And we needed no further proof that the government was pursuing Gibson.

Gibson finally opened the door and asked what James was doing there. They were in a city in the far south, a university center with many students and lecturers and guesthouses—it could not be a coincidence that James had arrived at his room.

But the government man gave no explanation. "Just traveling in the area," he said. "Do you want to get a beer?"

Gibson knew he could not refuse the offer. And from the bar on the first floor of the hotel, where they were seated, James ostentatiously made a telephone call. He said in a loud voice, "Hello! It's me. Yes, I am with him. There is no problem."

I received a text message that evening from Gibson. "My life is in danger. I think I may die tonight."

I thought about what Moses had said, about trying to flee the government within the country. Gibson's time was clearly limited—the police were using the country's journalists against one another. It was a form of repression: to turn against you the things and people you trusted, so that you had to fear your own people.

In a dictatorship one gained one's freedom not by defending the liberty of others but by working to diminish it; for each person you turned in you earned more space. Even if such freedom could not last, even if you could lose by betrayal what had been gained by betrayal, it was a kind of freedom: a negative freedom. People's innate desire to be free thus provided essential sustenance to repression, dictatorship.

James decided to take a room at Gibson's hotel. That night Gibson paid for his accommodation, but left discreetly to sleep in another lodging.

Early the following morning he boarded a bus for Kigali. He had nowhere to go, so I asked him to come home.

He looked disheveled. It was the toll of being on the run for two weeks. He had not eaten in several days, he said. And he was tired.

On the first day he just slept. From the night until the next evening. He then came out for a couple of hours, and went back to bed. I did not know if he actually slept, or if he was in some kind of trance-like state. He stepped out of his room looking ragged, in a strange condition, before again returning, without saying a word.

I had put him in the last room, at the end of the corridor. This room had large windows—with iron bars running across—over which we drew curtains. I told him that he was behind a bulletproof door: I pulled open the heavy door, slowly, as if to prove my point.

I was worried about disturbing Gibson. I did not play music, and made sure not to bang the doors. The house was silent.

I quickened with each move outside the house. Each car driving by, its engine growing louder and then diminishing. Each knock on the door, ring of the doorbell. There was a sense that Gibson, hidden in that last room, was being constantly hunted, and that slowly the entire city, outside our compound, was converging upon us, following his trail.

The following morning he emerged from his room in a rush—as if suddenly woken—and said that we had to make a plan. He ate two omelets with vegetables and a peanut-butter sandwich, and drank a large glass of milk. He said grace before eating. The morning passed without further conversation. Gibson seemed lost in thought. For lunch I heated up a homemade pizza, but he set aside the cheese-encrusted olives. "I have stopped eating things I don't recognize," he said. I ate one of the pieces he had set aside. "Oh, it's just an olive," he said, and he bit into a piece. I too thought he should move. And if Moses was correct we did not have much time.

This question of when the police might arrive made me worry—the station was just around the corner from my house. And we were only two or three blocks from the president's office. It was one of the safest parts of the city, but also one of the most observed.

Gibson walked noiselessly in the living room, a ghostlike figure moving along the walls and never lingering in the room's center. He stood by the windows and looked out, searching the landscape. But there was nothing to see. And only silence around us.

The gardener would come to water the plants. His quiet footsteps alarmed the journalist.

And in all this something was pushing a man to abandon his country. It was not an easy decision, nor obvious. There was something powerful and instinctual working on Gibson. The incidents, one after the other, had shown him clearly that he could not stay, that his country was no longer welcome to him. Everything he had connection to was now dangerous. He had been ripped out of society, of his world. He was stateless, homeless, being pursued. There were no more sanctuaries against the isolation and fear.

One evening he went back to his apartment to collect a few of his things. I waited nervously at home. He found his landlady in his room—and she began to scream at him, to say that she had thrown him out, that he was useless, what was he still doing here. She left saying she was going to fetch the police, that this was her duty. Gibson hurriedly packed some belongings and departed before she could return. He did not lock the apartment door. This—her sudden hysteria—was a signal of all that threatened.

He didn't even have time to feel what it was like in his apartment, he said. There was no time or space. The separations, one by one, were all wrenching.

That night in the house he sat on his bed, feet on the ground, praying. To his right, on a bedside table, was a small porcelain figurine of the Virgin Mary and her child. It was one of the things he had salvaged from his apartment. Next to his foot was a little suitcase on wheels, Chinese made, on top of which lay his frayed toothbrush. He opened his eyes. They were deep red. He did not speak. I offered him some rice. What would become of *New Horizons,* he asked, into which he had put so much work? And what about the girl he had wanted to marry? She would find someone more able to take care of her. He looked distressed, and shaken by the episode with the landlady. The police were now undoubtedly on his trail, and knew he was in Kigali. I felt close to his small figure. It was a hopeless position to be in, the individual pitted against the state; I felt his utter helplessness.

Umuseso had been shut down. It was official. The journalists from the newspaper had all fled, and weeks had gone by without a new issue. At a milk and yogurt café near my house, I asked the vendor what he thought. "A light has gone out in the country," he said. I sensed that the people felt they had been divorced from the power, that they were in the dark. They would only speak of *Umuseso*'s absence in private.

It was perhaps no coincidence that the closure of one of the last avenues of free speech in the country coincided with a surge in violence. This would be a turning point in the history of Rwanda. The regime had chosen: there was already no political opposition; but now the regime had begun to silence itself—it had chosen the path of greater repression. There was no longer a valve for dissenters, even within the party. The pressure could only build.

Moses would tell me that that moment, when *Umuseso* closed, was a new beginning—and a return to an older state of affairs in the country. It was the beginning of the *pensée unique.* Of a single way of thinking.

This term, the *pensée unique,* has a frightening history. It was in such an environment that the genocide was conducted. Such speed and efficiency were hardly known on this continent—or even in the world. But when the killing began there were almost no voices to oppose it. Those who did were imprisoned or killed. The single-minded dedication of a nation unable to think or say otherwise produced one of the greatest and most horrific crimes in a century.

And now, sixteen years on, people were being reminded of that time.

The genocide was also preceded by grenade attacks.

The hatred between ruler and ruled in Rwanda was old. But the *pensée unique* took this hatred to its logical limit. Just prior to the genocide newspapers were launched principally to flatter the government, and they would spur the killers on, and go to great lengths to debase the victims. Flattery was a symptom of the *pensée unique*. It is what replaced the voices that were dead.

Forbidden from speaking their minds, from asking questions, loyalty and fear took over. Ideas of good and evil, and people's convictions about them, became crystallized, and devastating. The genocide went far: mothers killed their children; men murdered their wives; neighbors killed each other; children hacked into their parents.

For this violence as well Rwanda is a remarkable country.

In the weeks following the explosion in the city center, grenades had continued to go off in the capital—and they finally grew too many to be denied. The bodies had been seen; the people were talking. The government, silent, risked losing its credibility and aura of power. The president was forced to mention it at his press conferences.

The explosions thus became real, and were allowed to enter the world. In this place perception was commanded by the president, not by one's eyes and ears and nose and skin.

The regime had given new cause for unease: a succession of senior officials, including those close to the president—his chiefs of cabinet, ministers, ambassadors, judicial and military and intelligence officers—had fled the country over the past years, saying they had feared for their lives. But the insecurity reached a height when the country's top general, who for many years had led bloody campaigns on behalf of the president, and still retained the loyalty of a large part of the army, deserted. There was a sense of panic in the country, though public expression was suppressed, still calm.

The paranoia became acute because the president and his men were a minority within a minority in power. This general who had fled, Kayumba, was from an elite that had fractured. The president could no longer trust many of those who had grown up with him as refugees, who had fought for him in the liberation war. The threat was on the inside of his government.

Kayumba was felt by many to be the president's successor. He was admired for having fought on the front lines with the soldiers; the president, the strategic mind, had always stayed in the headquarters. To isolate the general, get him out of the way, the president had named him the ambassador to India. But on a visit to Kigali the general was interrogated by the president's men, and sensed the distrust. Just before he was to meet with the president one morning he fled to South Africa and sought asylum.

People were suddenly afraid to speak the general's name. On the streets, in bars, they referred to him as "*lui,* him," or "*wa mugabo,* that man." And they were saying that the president's opponents—so far, mostly civilian dissidents—had now gained an army.

The signs of the hardening of the government multiplied. The newspapers' language became high-pitched. "Enemy of the State." "Terrorist." "Traitor." Such language the people of Rwanda also recognized from before the genocide. Stories insulting the officials who had fled became regular in the press, along with large pictures of the president shaking hands with the powerful—Bill Gates, Tony Blair and Bill Clinton.

The body of a former collaborator of Kayumba was exhumed by the authorities in the capital. This man had died some time ago, but a doubt had arisen as to whether the burial had been faked. Digging up the man's grave was apparently the only measure that would prove he was not alive.

The army saw its salary increased. The presidential guard had its pay almost doubled.

And at a press conference the president at last acknowledged the fears. "Nobody can carry out a coup d'état. Never! Please!" But he was visibly agitated; he was furious that his generals would disobey and turn against him. He guaranteed the country's security. His army was one of the most powerful and merciless in Africa. "Sleep well," he told his people.

On the night before Gibson was to leave, we stood outside my house, in the dark, and watched the capital. From our vantage point we could see across the shrouded valley: cars moved left and right along the high road carved into the facing hill.

After days of silence Gibson was in a talkative mood. There was some annoyance in his voice, some impatience, some agony. He resented having to leave behind the country he had grown up in and that he loved. He had believed in his country, its future.

His fate, to him, seemed unjust.

"Have you noticed?" he said, suddenly.

"Noticed what?"

He pointed in front of us. "The lights. Have you seen anything like them?" He paused. I was not quite sure what he meant, but I looked carefully at the orange sodium-vapor points, followed them both ways along the road.

"You grew up in Dubai, yes?" I nodded at him. "Have you

noticed the space between the street lights? Tell me, are they this close in Dubai?"

I had not remarked this before.

"No. Certainly not," I said after some thought. I asked him how he knew about the lighting in Dubai. He had seen it on photographs and, adjusting for scale, had compared the distance.

He went on: "You would think from the street lights that Rwanda is a resource-rich country. But only four percent of Rwanda's people have electricity in their houses. *Four percent!* How incredible. But this is the first thing visitors see. And this is impressive, they are stunned by the small country in Africa that has come through a genocide, and now has such roads, such lights."

I asked him what he thought of the lights.

"Wait a little," Gibson said. "Look at the bottom of the hill. Below the line of streetlamps. Do you see that it is all black in the valley? What is there?"

I absorbed the effect of his tone, clear, direct—appealing. Gibson wanted to communicate something important, something dear to him. I stayed attentive to his every word.

"Ordinary people live there. They live in that blackness. And now again look at the street." The sudden light, its brightness, mildly hurt the eye. "You see the cars driving up and down. Do you see people?"

There were none. Not one.

"So where are the people?"

I was not sure. What was he trying to tell me? And then slowly I became aware to a noise. The shuffling of feet, the murmur of voices, the hushing of loose clothes swaying over thin bodies. I turned to look down our street, which did not have lights, and was utterly dark. It was a cobblestone street, treacherous in the night—I had often tripped over the stones and nearly fallen. And the road was on the edge of a steep hill without a fence. One could easily slip down the slope. Yet the people had chosen this road. It was the hour when work ended, and men and women were making their way home, walking at a measured pace, using their weight, throwing their weight forward and sending their legs ahead like a crutch, to climb our hill. A sea of people were making their way up.

"Why do they walk in the dark? You would think we would use these wonderful new roads we have been given—isn't this development, progress? But no. Ah, look at this road! Anyone can see this for himself! And you begin to understand our country. We the poor, we are like the insects, scared of the lights. We hide from the government, which wants to see us all the time. So you now see that the truth in our country is hidden, and you need to look not for what is there, but for what they hide. You cannot pay attention to what they show you, but need to listen to those who are kept quiet. You need to look differently in a dictatorship, you need to think about how to listen to people who live in fear."

I was stunned by this road before me, brilliantly lit, empty, that seemed almost burned into the hill. I had seen it every day, but had never really seen it.

These were the roads that the government had used every day to track down Gibson's whereabouts.

Gibson was still frowning. And he was restless, no doubt from the journey ahead the next day.

I asked if there was some alternative to him fleeing—we could ask at the foreign embassies. They had influence with the president, and could perhaps force back the government repression. I wanted to know if I was condemned to losing my closest friend in Rwanda, and if the country was condemned to losing one of its most capable and promising journalists.

But the problem with Gibson's case was that it was not official—if the government had pursued him through the courts, through some public mechanism, there might have been a chance. But they had gone after him in secret, extrajudicially. "That is when you really have to be afraid. They will starve you, beat you, hurt you until they get what they want. It isn't for nothing that all the other *Umuseso* journalists have fled. It would be foolish to hope that they will treat me fairly. And the embassies always listen to the government. They always believe what the president says."

I felt his irritation was not just at me, but also at his situation.

He said, "Will we meet again, my friend?"

I understood the question signified much more. I murmured, "Of course."

He put his left hand on my palm. "I wish I could stop what is happening to me. It will not be good." Without looking at him I could tell he had begun to weep. It seemed that he needed to let out the emotions that he had been holding within for so long.

He knew that leaving the country was no guarantee: those who had fled before him had not found escape. Some had been shot in broad daylight near their new homes. The Rwandan government had a secret service with great reach. Gibson knew that it was likely that he would still be pursued, that his flight would be long and difficult and that through most of it he would be alone; it was imaginable now that he could die without anyone knowing.

He was going to sell his sofa, the pathetic sofa set that I had sat on, to put together funds for his journey. I sensed both his resignation, and his attachment to the hope that he would one day make his own home. The sofa was as much a symbol of a dream: it would receive visitors, and perhaps the girl he loved; it might still be there when he founded a family.

I didn't think he would get much for the sofa anyway. I gave him some money without him asking for it.

Gibson would take a combination of buses as army officers ran many transport companies. If he bought a ticket directly to the border from Kigali the authorities would more easily catch him.

And the next morning as he made to leave, with his small suitcase and in his simple clothes, looking cleaner than he had in the past weeks because he had shaved, he gave me a brief hug and for a moment met my eyes. There was a vagueness in his gaze, as if he were already lost. His feet moved uncertainly and he struggled with the suitcase. His head turned in every direction. I asked him a question; he nodded unthinkingly. He seemed like someone who did not himself know where he was going. He was overwhelmed. And so this man, who had never before been outside Rwanda, stepped like this, an outcast, shorn of his country by his own government, into the world.

Not long after, I was at a diplomatic event in which European parliaments pledged to give the Rwandan government more than $300 million.

The ambassador of the European Union spoke on the podium of the strong partnership he was forging with Rwanda, saying he was profoundly pleased with the government's policies, that he hoped Europe could be of further assistance as the government continued its important work.

The ambassador, furthermore, announced that this new money would go directly to the Rwandan government's coffers for it to spend as it saw fit. The national machinery that the government was building and using on the people required vast sums of money. And much of this money came from Western governments. The goal of their aid to Rwanda was to develop the country and prevent another outbreak of violence. It was for this purpose that Western governments financed the roads, the police, the agriculture and health systems, all of which were cited as improvements in Rwanda under the president. Yet they also served as the instruments of repression.

The police were said to protect the population; they also tortured. The roads were said to increase mobility; yet they also enabled the government to control the people. Dissidents were denied health care that those who kept quiet were given. The Intore were assured of jobs.

The event was held on the lawns of the ambassador's mansion in the city, and it brought together officials and their wives from the various embassies as well as senior government officers. Waiters served wine, each with one arm behind his back. Guests ate slivers of salmon on creamed toast. There were smiles across the garden. It was a victory for the government to have obtained this new round of financing, crucial for it to continue to hold power and execute its ideas.

The Western embassy officials were also pleased that they had managed to obtain so much money from their parliaments. Rwanda, in return for the foreign support, did its best to behave as a model international citizen, sending police officers to Haiti for earthquake relief and soldiers to Darfur as U.N. peacekeepers.

A ministry official took the podium and did not thank the European ambassador. He said that to avoid misquoting he would be reading out a letter from the foreign minister. Wiping the sweat off his forehead with a kerchief, he read a speech in which the government said it appreciated that the world had realized Rwanda was capable of overseeing its own finances, resources and people as it felt necessary.

It was a new kind of foreign aid, designed to empower countries to be responsible for their own development. Recipient governments assured the donor nations that their policies were designed and carried out in the interests of their people, and that the money was well spent.

I found the ambassador standing on some footsteps, surrounded by his underlings—functionaries, secretaries. A number of other ambassadors came by to shake his hand, offer their congratulations and express support for that evening's announcement.

I shook the ambassador's hand as well. He was a plump man, going bald. The officials around him did not speak much: the ambassador seemed to be holding court, jovially telling the others that after his Rwanda posting he would probably be consigned to a European garden where the ex-ambassadors, without functions but still on the diplomatic payroll, smoked cigars and reminisced. "I shudder to think about that place," he said, but with a smile, so one knew that it would not be quite as bad as he was making out. He looked at me strangely.

"I'm curious," I said, after I confirmed the amount of money he was giving the Rwandan government. "This is not a loan, but charity. Where does the money come from?"

"European taxpayers," he said. "That's where all our money comes from."

"Aren't you worried about giving money to a dictator?"

He bristled a little, and his aides shrank away.

He could have sent me off, but the ambassador seemed in the mood for confrontation. "I have no problem with giving money to a dictator."

"That's a bold statement," I said. "Especially coming from Europe, you know very well what a dictatorship is capable of."

He shrugged. "He runs one of the most effective governments in Africa. I'm proud to be giving him money."

"But you're financing repression."

"Where's the proof?"

"I know a journalist who needs your help. He's being pursued by the government right now, and is fleeing for his life. Can you help him?"

"The government is fixing its problems with the journalists. Wait and see."

"And meanwhile you give them hundreds of millions of dollars?"

"By giving money we influence their policies. We are for freedom of speech. We will influence the government in the right direction."

"Well, do it soon. I'm trying my best to keep the journalists going, but there aren't many left in the country to work with. Would you be able to help them? I personally know a reporter who fled just a few days ago. There are others like him. I've been following their cases. I know how the government does it. They're fleeing the country, fearing for their lives. I can arrange for them to speak to you if you need proof."

"We know all this; we don't need to meet them," he said, waving a hand to say that he was done with me.

A Rwandan official came by and the ambassador opened his arms to welcome her. He had returned to his jovial self.

I walked home, this time taking a well-lit street. It was desolate, and I missed Gibson.

After the dissident general Kayumba's departure, the government ordered the army out of its camps to replace the police on the streets. The soldiers patrolled in groups of four or five, across the country. Their automatic weapons were not slung over their shoulders, as one might expect in an initial deployment— but held firmly in both arms, their fingers pressed against the triggers.

We learned that in preparation for the election, in towns and villages, mayors and small officials had been purged and replaced with men of or loyal to the army. The country, at its most minute levels, was being systematically militarized.

Power was inverted. At the highest government positions the president would sometimes make a show of accommodating rivals, so the world would see him as sharing power. But the repression was moved to the level of the villages, where only those devoted to the president were installed as administrators. In this way the individual had little hope of liberty. Even if a leader in the capital created an opposition party, no citizen in the countryside would dare to oppose the president.

The classroom was diminished both in number and vitality. Those journalists who had served as role models in this dangerous and oppressive environment were gone. And now it was much more difficult to get the others to talk.

The fast chopping of the helicopter passed above from time to time. I sat in the office garden, under the guava tree and its white flowers. I thought of Gibson, and how he had left. I was not going to let this go without a struggle. I felt I needed to recruit.

So many people had already given up so much for their freedom in this country.

The main story in the papers at this time was about the country's junior football team, many of whose players had been born after the genocide, and their success in a tournament. There was a story about an exhibition organized by the American embassy where one could purchase African baskets and beads. There was something about how the genocide survivors appreciated the memorials. And an article quoted a senior U.N. official who stated that Rwanda was an example to the world, and that its success in managing its affairs and people should be replicated by other countries.

FORCE

The repression grew after Gibson departed. We tried to save the training program.

Agnès, the fiery girl from our class who had survived a term in prison, was among the first we would lose.

Those who had tried had failed. It was no longer possible to find reasonable voices in the country. The press had been decimated in its widest sense, and profoundly. Newspapers were meaningless: merely repeating government propaganda, publishing public announcements, inventing flattery. News was replaced by funny stories, anecdotal, distracting, little colorful reports on the radio. There was a report about the government donating cows to villagers. About students pleased with government scholarships. A girl had won a beauty competition. The news was empty, deceptive—listening to it one would think the country was at ease. And the frivolity of the tone of the news during the widespread repression had become frightening.

Some Rwandan academics were trying to dialogue with the president's office, to calm the government's paranoia, stem the growing distrust. But they were ignored, and only allowed to talk as long as they were deemed harmless. The president's words had become the news, indeed were becoming the sole voice in the country.

The repression polarized the journalists. The few dissenting voices that remained were extreme, riven with anger. They wrote in independent news outlets that received little advertising and few contributors. The government arrested them; they emerged from detention centers even more rabid, even more isolated, and consigned to the fringes. Unable to talk, the country's journalists had begun to scream. The last free journalists began to self-destruct.

And the government held these rabid reporters up as proof of a need for greater repression. Other journalists were held up as models: those whom the president invited to his press conferences, around whose flattery he felt comfortable. The free, independent voices were denied information, stood up by the government, made to wait hours for interviews, disdained; they became the wretched. The "important" journalists the president happily spoke to for hours.

It amplified the frustration. The free voices were isolated—and in their solitude only grew more furious.

The fear was growing. There was a sense of terror in the dissenting reports. And there was even greater terror as they were silenced, as praise of the president became more widespread, more intense, more total.

Agnès fell into the trap. More and more upset, she began to write in her newspaper about the most forbidden aspects of the president's repression: about the hate that still existed from the genocide and the president's killings. These were things everyone knew and spoke about in private, but that they knew not to report, even to vehemently deny in public. Agnès had decided to take on the government.

I tried to tell her that she was succumbing to the government's repression, that this was precisely what the authorities were hoping for. I told her that though I sympathized—it was natural to want to give vent to the anger and sense of injustice—she had to think about her place in society: that she was more useful alive than dead, more useful free than arrested, more effective as part of a group, carefully choosing the stories she covered and always reporting the government's position even if it was a blatant lie. But she did not listen. And she stopped coming to the classes.

We lost a good many journalists from our class in this fashion—seduced by the anger and violence, they were taken into the path of confrontation. The students incited one another. A girl one day refused to accept the certificates I was handing out to attest that the students had completed a training module. She came up to the front of the class and turned to face the students, before beginning to accuse me: "You! I can see through your deception. You are really a pro-government man. Why are you telling us to report on hospitals and disease rates when the real problems in this country are political? What are you really here to do? You are keeping us away from the issues that matter in our lives by making us write these insignificant reports."

I didn't know what to tell her. Her emotion was damning, making it difficult for me to respond or defend myself.

I wanted the students to avoid an offensive against the government, despite all that had happened to their colleagues. I thought that if they waited they might find an opening. Perhaps they knew better than I did about the government's intentions: perhaps they saw there was no hope that the government would change its methods. In this case the only avenue was revolution. But the students needed training—they were not ready to confront the more serious issues in the country. They had first to make mistakes with the more innocuous items.

I was also bound by the Western governments funding our program. The money we received was an insignificant fraction of the hundreds of millions of dollars they gave the government. But the donors wanted on no account to confront the government even with our small sum. I was forced to use only officially permitted topics like "poverty reduction." It was my hope that the students would benefit from this training more fully one day, when they obtained their freedom.

But there was no telling this to the students—more difficult to address because they were poorer in knowledge and experience than the older batch; indeed, the quality of our new students had noticeably begun to drop. And now many of those with any conviction—the most important of qualities for the reporter, particularly in such a dangerous environment—were lost to the easy satisfaction that anger offered.

As with Agnès, I tried desperately to convince others to remain in our program, but they were unable to think beyond the logic of immediate action. They seemed to feel they were advancing some sort of revolution: that by exposing all the repression of the government at once, by speaking about the disappearances of workers, politicians, friends, brothers and sisters, they would be able to force change. They wanted to speak; it was as if the violence that the government had operated on their communities had become unbearable. And in this state it was difficult to convince them to stay quiet for a little longer. Students abandoned their homework about vasectomy and malnutrition in the countryside and began to write rabid, political reports for the marginal newspapers that they had set up.

The girl who shouted at me soon left. I heard she was working for a paper, then at a radio station, and was fired by both.

There was an aspect of self-defense in their insistent journalism. Continuing to report was a way to protect their society and themselves: the students knew that if they stopped writing, no one would, and the threat would be greater. So their decision to confront the government, and to what extent, had to be a personal choice.

I did what I could to protect the students. I told them to call me should any of them change their minds, or need help. Our classroom was a place of learning and always open. I felt sad and guilty when they left.

Their departures I felt also exposed us. The classroom became a place of bleakness; I too felt lost. I felt that the real combat was being waged outside, that we were in a useless exercise with unrealistic hopes, that we were weak for confronting the repression obliquely and not openly and courageously like the other students.

It was not long after I had helped Gibson flee the country. Roger, the man I had met at the conference, who had laughed beneath the portrait of the president, called one afternoon.

"You never kept your promise," he said, accusingly.

"Who is this?"

"You don't even remember."

It took me a little while to recall. And I only did when he started to laugh, his hysterical high-pitched laugh. I felt embarrassed. I said I had been busy since we had last met, and that it had not been intentional.

"I believe you."

Roger said he would like to meet. Still feeling apologetic, I suggested getting together at a pizzeria.

It was in the city center, in a complex of buildings that included a skyscraper under construction said to belong to the president. People swarmed the entryway, lit by neon tubes. On a countertop in plastic bowls were pastries, slices of pizza, quiches and other fattening foods. An Indian entrepreneur who ran the restaurant hovered over the cash register. The crowd made a low hubbub: the place was popular among families, which made it ideal for a conversation.

The waitresses were Rwandan, all young women. One of them came to take our order. The lights were dull and steady.

Roger said he had already eaten. I wondered if it was true, or if he was being *infura*. This was the local notion of dignity. Gluttony was a particularly egregious sin—it was said that an *infura* could starve to death on a neighbor's porch but not admit that he was hungry. Roger was eyeing the menu. I told him a slice of pizza and a soft drink would not be too much.

Roger was thin, scrawnier than I had first noticed. The veins on his bald head showed. His lips were thick, darkly colored. And he always seemed to bow his head a little while raising his shoulders, as if nervous.

"I just want to let you know up front," he said, "that we are being watched."

I raised my eyebrows.

"They are following me everywhere. See that man there, don't look now," he said. "Sorry, I couldn't say it on the phone."

There was a man sitting alone, without food or drink, at a table not far from us. I became angry for having exposed myself. I considered leaving at once.

He sensed it. "You shouldn't worry," he said. "I am in their good books for the moment."

I asked what he meant.

"They think I can still be saved," he said. "They have offered me a job."

"With whom?"

"The government paper."

"You're a journalist."

He told me he ran a blog that was critical of the government. It had published news about the dissident general, which was forbidden.

"But I used to be one of them," he said. "I am a defector."

My curiosity was piqued.

"I am not old enough to remember the previous regime. I grew up under the authority of the president, believing every word he said. I was even a child soldier in his army in 1991, was willing to give my life for him. I was only fourteen years old."

"What changed?"

"I grew up. I saw. This is not the country he spoke of. My friends didn't give up their lives for this. We have no justice in our country, no parliament, only one man with all the power. We have no independence, no freedom, even to think."

I wondered what this man, Roger, wanted from me.

He looked around the restaurant anxiously. "What do you feel? I don't want to take the job, but I need to make a living. I am studying law at university, part-time. It's hard as a student."

"The salary must be very good."

"They are trying to buy me off. But it's possible I can do better work from the inside. You know, fight from the inside." He looked up at me as though seeking confirmation.

"You can forget about being a journalist once you take that job," I said.

"Can *you* find me a job?"

I said I could try to help him, but could not guarantee it.

"There's a lot going on that's not being said. The government doesn't want it exposed."

"I agree," I said.

"We didn't live through a genocide to get another dictatorship. It's depressing."

Behind us three men were leaning over a counter and watching a music video, their faces almost plastered to the screen. Bikini-clad women, legs bronzed, drank brightly colored cocktails by a pool. "Ah, that's the life," one of the men said. "When will we have that in our country?"

"Maybe in 2020," said the other. "The president has said so." "Vision 2020" was a government mantra that had become a household word. The new roads, schools and hospitals built with Western aid: they were all part of a plan by the government to make Rwanda a middle-income country in the next decade. The idea had been borrowed from China and Singapore. Money would render the repression acceptable; and the people had given their allegiance in exchange for the dream of wealth.

"Don't believe what people tell you about our country," Roger said.

"One of my journalists left to become a presidential propagandist a few days after he was speaking in the class for freedom."

"This is a bullshit country," he said. "Bullshit! There is no truth." And he started to laugh strangely again.

"They will tell you that people here are free," he said. "Look around you, at the rich people of our country shopping, eating."

The pizza had arrived, but Roger let the food go cold. I bit into my slice, and watched him.

"You know," he said, "people are only free when they are not." Again he chuckled. "You see what I mean?" He laughed, and pointed at his head. "The control is here," he said, raising his eyebrows. "Once you are controlled here, then they let you walk around like you are free."

I watched his face intently. What a funny, peculiar man. He seemed a little off.

"Don't believe them!" he said. "You know they are rounding up people. You know this is happening. They are being detained in secret and tortured for colluding with the enemy. I know, I know!"

He started to eat. Then he giggled, with food in his mouth. "The government thinks I have information. That's why they want to buy me off," he said, with his mouth full.

"Bullshit country," I said.

He started to laugh. "You got it!" Now he became serious. "The job. Tell me what I should do."

"I sincerely don't know," I said. "It has to be your choice, your conviction."

He leaned back at this, and seemed to reflect seriously.

"Yes, we have to go slowly here," he said. "There is too much tension, too many angry words."

He left a piece of his pizza uneaten on the plate. The same with his soft drink, a part of it left in the bottle. "You know, all that has been built—the roads, the new skyscraper, the eight percent growth in the economy—it's been built by the military, and it's all great," he said. "What we need today is democracy. But every time I write something the president's office summons me. Now it's that enemy general. Am I working for him, they ask, just because I question their policies."

"What do they think of people like you?"

He shrugged. "In this place, secrets are everything. Secrets are how you build relationships. They are power. What is his name? Even that is a threat. There are laws against 'laughing at others' misfortune' and 'provoking ill feelings.' How to enforce such laws without looking into, even possessing, someone's soul? You know a few years ago we were very close to war with Uganda. I was very happy, because I knew I would pass my night in their capital."

I did not interrupt his meanderings, the intensity of the mood. "I want three things," he continued. "Peace in our country, the freedom to think and speak and democracy. Give me these three and I will be happy."

There was a clicking sound above us as the voltage fluctuated. The clicking stopped.

It was then that I had a flash of understanding about Roger. I had a sudden sense about him—the strange laugh, the perception, the flood of words—of isolation. I felt he had experienced a profound seclusion, living in such thoughts alone. It could happen in a dictatorship. And it was why he seemed such a misfit, so odd.

I had already seen something of such isolation. As I ate my last slices of pizza I felt again the melancholy of Gibson's loss. I thought of our time together, and of some of our happy moments.

The man followed Roger out.

.   .   .

Our fortune in the class seemed to turn when I recruited a journalist. He was a catch, possibly the best in the country at the time.

I was incessantly making a tour of conferences and events, searching for possible new students: I was combing the city for some last sign of courage, some willingness to speak. It was a hopeless exercise. The meetings were long and silent. The journalists merely listened, as if receiving instructions from officials on what to report. I moved from building to building solemnly, fatigued, and was about to give up on my efforts, when at an election event the government had organized to "inform" journalists how to report on the vote, I saw a young man stand up and ask:

"Excuse me, sirs, but in the name of our National Electoral Commission, we don't have the word 'independent.' Is our commission independent or is it run by the government?"

In any other place it might have been an ordinary question, but in Rwanda, in this environment, at this moment, it took a certain audacity to raise the issue. People in the audience turned around. Indeed, the National Electoral Commission, also financed by Western governments, was not independent—but no one, not even the foreign donors who knew well what they were financing, had publicly pointed this out.

It had fallen on a Rwandan to do so. The official maneuvered around the question, not really answering it. And like much dissent in Rwanda, the idea was buried, passed over.

I asked around, and found out that the young man had in fact recently been hired by Jean-Bosco, who was now working in exile. Together they were running a news website that had replaced the paper the government had shut down. This connection to a former student—and one who had challenged the government—instilled confidence. I learned the young man's name was Jean-Léonard.

I presented myself to him in the parking lot. The government event was nearly finished—he was leaving early. He had heard of our training program, knew some of our other students, and said he admired our work. Jean-Léonard was a soft-spoken man, but with a quickness of tongue, and exuding a kind of charisma. I had seen the authority he had commanded in the audience. He now spoke to me with concentration and urgency.

"The government is using more and more force," he said, with a slight stammer. "But who will stand up for us? There is only one voice, one way of thinking."

He didn't feel that the other students were wrong to go on the offensive, and think of a revolution in speech—to breach the enveloping quietness in the country. He said they were on a dangerous mission, and would quickly need support.

His face was shaped like a half moon, and when he smiled it gave the impression both of docility and friendliness. Now he looked at me, as though he had said what had to be said, and was waiting for a reaction.

I wondered if Jean-Léonard might be convinced to take a larger role in our group, to become something of a lead practitioner, to train the other students and perhaps offer them work experience at his website.

I was hoping to renew a sense of leadership in the class. And I wanted someone from within their cadre. The apprehension had become quite extreme: someone like Jean-Léonard would be an obvious inspiration to the students.

The difficulty was in the training. There were almost no outlets left in the country where the students could experience proper journalism—the process of conceiving of a story on one's own, investigating it independently, developing the ideas, and working to a conclusion that one had been unaware of at the beginning. This was crucial, to allow one's mind to remain open so this new conclusion could find expression.

I did not think the students would understand this point in theoretical terms. They needed to experience the process, needed to feel the sensation of allowing a new idea to emerge and find freedom.

The truth-finding process was becoming alien in the country; and in time, without the ability for renewal, it could be buried, potentially eliminated.

Only a few small, independent news outlets remained, each run by one or two journalists. Agnès and Jean-Léonard were almost alone in their endeavor. We needed to bring everyone together into a cohesive group.

I had high hopes for the new recruit, and what he would do for the students, and for the journalists in the country.

I remembered Jean-Léonard's last words to me: about the *pensée unique*. And I wondered why, despite his quietness of speech, he had seemed somehow agitated.

The classes were in the meantime becoming harder to

endure. I was finding it difficult to get through to the students. But there seemed, from their responses, still to be time for intervention. There was still some pride.

I was annoyed with Moses.

During the lunch break I took the two taxi-buses to his home, in a poor part of town, where the houses were all of tin roofs at odd angles, set against one another. I found him in a small room, watching a Brazilian soap opera on his laptop.

"Was it you who invited the National AIDS Commission man to the class as a new student?" I asked.

"Yes."

"But he's not a journalist. He writes for the government commission website."

"He's not so bad," Moses said. "That's all we can get now."

I was sullen. "It's becoming difficult in the classroom. They're coming from a long way off," I said.

Moses returned to his soap opera. He was evidently not in the mood for a discussion about this. Sometimes he fell into his depressions about the genocide, and was impossible to raise from his stupor.

He said these moods came involuntarily, and they were not accompanied by any great trauma—rather, he fell into a state of uncaring. It was what he called being a "walking dead."

I returned to the class and found the students staring at a newspaper's center spread. It was printed in color, which was rare, for it was expensive. I drew closer. The students said the report praised a government official. I looked at the top, and felt disgust when I saw Cato's name.

The plan for that day was to discuss how to report on the election. The students all wanted to criticize the government— but about how not enough arrangements had been made to allow people to vote. I asked if anyone was going to mention the right not to vote.

The students squirmed. "It is a national duty."

"Can you *not* vote in this country?"

"They will accuse us of being against the government if we write that."

"The president has declared that we must all vote."

A student explained: "The president has ordered that he be re-elected with a massive turnout. Everyone must go out to vote. It will prove that the whole country is behind him."

So their criticism of the government was a kind of show; it was criticism sanctioned by the government itself. Pointing out the lack of arrangements would help people obey the government's order to vote.

The president excelled at creating a façade of democracy to conceal his repression. Rwanda had more political parties than most democracies, more newspapers and radio stations, more officials fired for corruption. And now it would have a stellar election turnout.

It made the repression difficult to decipher through statistics. One had to rely on people's experiences—but even those were growing more distant, becoming harder to access.

"Will you obey the president's order?" I asked. "Is there a way to indicate what is going on?"

Someone said, "How can we do that without risking our security?"

The students shuffled. They knew what the president was accomplishing. I wanted to offer a realistic solution. "Could we cite the law?" I said. "It's stated that people have electoral rights. The president himself has approved this."

I had perhaps touched a nerve by laying out the president's blatant hypocrisy. A young man said he would investigate whether people had been properly informed about the electoral law. He might subtly send a message about the government's order in a benign story listing people's testimonies.

I thought this was a clever approach. I asked for other ideas.

A woman proposed a more precise but ambitious story along similar lines. She said that the government had started a competition for the election. Those villages that voted most resoundingly for the president would receive rewards for their loyalty. She would find a mayor willing to confess this.

It was possible that the students were bouncing between the government and their teacher—caught between trying to please one and the other. It was a mentality in dictatorship: the need to please and flatter one's superior. But I felt for them to say the words was a step forward. What we needed now was some conviction, solidarity. And perhaps, with some creativity, we could have a wave of safe but inherently truthful reports.

Jean-Léonard was shot dead. It happened late in the evening as he was driving home. The gunmen killed him in his car.

That morning he had published a report about the dissident general, Kayumba, who had five days earlier been shot in the streets of Johannesburg. The government of course denied having anything to do with it: Rwandan newspapers began in lockstep to report how Johannesburg was such a dangerous city, and how Lucky Dube, a reggae star, had been killed there in a street shooting. But Jean-Léonard had information, obtained from within the government, linking the president's immediate entourage—those who reported directly to him—to the attack on the general.

Kayumba had escaped. A burly man, veteran of many of the president's wars, he wrestled with his assailant despite the bullet wound in his abdomen. An official South African investigation discovered links to the Rwandan government. Reports indicated the hit man, once captured, had tried to bribe the Johannesburg police with a large amount of cash.

South Africa was at the time hosting the football World Cup—Africa's first. It did not appreciate the negative publicity. Diplomatic relations with Rwanda soured.

Jean-Léonard had paid the price for speaking up with his life.

His funeral, in the city, was a silent affair. A number of obvious government agents—strange figures unknown to Jean-Léonard's friends and his wife, who was trying to comfort their two-year-old daughter—were sent to monitor those who attended, and also to signal that the repression was unfinished.

The classroom was silent. There was no more initiative to take on the government, there were no discussions even when I tried. Sometimes I felt that I was talking to the air. The students now seemed to have lost hope.

And one afternoon, when it was time for lunch and when we all usually walked to a cheap restaurant around the corner, for its local-style buffet, I saw the students go in the other direction, toward the main road.

There, a black Mercedes had been parked at the curb. It was Cato, the Intore journalist. He was wearing dark glasses and leaning out of his window, one arm resting on the top of the glass and the other on his steering wheel. The car was new, as were his suit and fashion accessories. He was evidently doing well in his propaganda job. The journalists crowded around his car with interest, and he started to talk with them, gesticulating animatedly. I think he saw me from the corner of his eye.

I turned and walked up the dusty road to the restaurant with two students who decided to come along. Over lunch I looked at them, at their young and emaciated faces that still showed idealism, and I felt immensely sorry that they were so principled.

The main news in the local and international press about Rwanda that week was that Ban Ki-moon, the United Nations secretary-general, had chosen Rwanda's president to lead a special high-profile committee that would aim to improve the welfare of people worldwide. The president would chair a group that included the Microsoft co-founder and philanthropist Bill Gates, the Nobel Prize winner Muhammad Yunus and the media magnate Ted Turner. The group was meant to bring together distinguished voices in favor of development for the poor; it would devise ways to improve people's lives. Ban said the committee would be a collection of development "superheroes." A number of messages of congratulations for Kagame came in from foreign leaders and dignitaries. The president said in response that he was honored.

The more the president's statements went unchallenged by Rwandan journalists and citizens, the more the world believed in their truth. The government's propaganda was being made into a successful export. The killing of Jean-Léonard and the government's massacres had been reported abroad by the United Nations, human rights organizations and the international media. But these voices found ever fewer echoes within Rwanda, and began to seem disconnected and almost unreal.

A few days later I received more disturbing news. Agnès was arrested after she wrote an article titled "It Is Not the King Who Kills, but His Courtiers." This was a well-known proverb from the time of the Rwandan monarchy. Agnès had linked the government to Jean-Léonard's killing, and also written about the massacres committed by the president's forces during the genocide. Agnès' paper was a tiny affair, privately printed and with limited circulation. But the president did not tolerate insolence. It was unclear what the government would do with Agnès. Her colleague was also arrested, along with a young man who had attended a few of our classes. The man was allegedly responsible for a digitally altered image of the president that gave him a mustache like Hitler's.

I tried to reach Agnès but was unable to get through. She was being kept somewhere, perhaps in a detention center, beyond reach.

But one day she called me. She did not ask for help, money or any specific support. I was ready to recommend a lawyer, though I was persuaded it would do nothing to help her in a dictator's courts: the single law that mattered was the president's word. An order would come from his office that would determine her fate. "I am preparing myself for another term in prison," Agnès said solemnly. I suppose she felt something like a martyr—that she had known implicitly what was to happen and that she had felt it was the only possible outcome for her.

I was shocked. I searched for Moses, and found him in the office, his eyes red.

"They've got the core of the journalists now," Moses said. "The imbeciles."

The government subsequently produced two peasants whom it accused of having killed Jean-Léonard. We only heard their names. Even cattle thieves were paraded on national television, but these men were not shown to us. One began to wonder if they existed; but of course they did. It was no surprise. The men even confessed to murdering the journalist—as an act of revenge, they claimed, for someone Jean-Léonard had supposedly killed during the genocide.

It was routine government method to smear those it considered enemies. In this way a ministry official who had noted some problems with government policies was accused of raping his employee. A man who had saved people during the genocide was accused of having run a racket to extort money from them. A political rival of the president was accused of aiding terrorists. Someone who had become too successful could be accused, out of pure jealousy, of harboring corrupt ideas. The government used rumor to advance its purpose. Without justice, without any means to defend oneself, if the government wanted you it was easy to create a crime; and the accused were often too afraid even to point out that the proof had been fabricated.

Often, they either submitted to the government or fled.

The powerful and petty, from all strata of society, backgrounds, religions and ethnicities had over the years run away from their country—like Gibson, and like the president's family half a century ago, when a prior government had chased away people of their ethnicity.

The journalists said the involvement of the peasants in Jean-Léonard's affair was a signal. The government had been so brazen as to accuse these insignificant and arbitrary men to show the population how powerful it was.

The authorities could make anyone confess to any crime. They could make anyone say anything. The theater and fear of dictatorship were being escalated.

Anyone who could be associated with the dissident general Kayumba was rounded up at this time. The government was, as always, ruthless in seeking out the enemy: the slightest suspicion could mean you were forced off the streets to an undisclosed location. To your family, you had simply "disappeared."

The general's brother, a government soldier once close to the president, began to be threatened, accused of crimes, as were other members of the general's family still in Rwanda. Officially they were free people. One knew to avoid them.

News stories were careful to avoid mentioning a connection to the general, or even to South Africa—which was difficult because the football World Cup was under way and it would have been natural for citizens to follow stories in that country. Everyone listened attentively for a word from the president, or from the government radio, about what it was possible to say without risk.

There was a new set of explosions in Rwanda. It was ascertained that the grenades had been thrown from the backs of motorcycles. The government first blamed them on Rwandan rebels based in Congo, and then on General Kayumba, who it said was collaborating with those rebels.

The explosions were used as audacious signs of defiance. The grenades were thrown near crowded bus stations and markets, but into empty spaces. They became a signal to the president that the attackers were toying with him, and that they could easily cause much greater destruction.

Homes were sacked and people detained in secret prisons. Then the country's most powerful generals were placed under house arrest one after the other, suspected of loyalty to Kayumba.

Fear had spread in the president's inner circles. Everyone was suspected of treachery, and this sense of suspicion—as everything that the president felt—filtered down into society.

It was what could happen. The population of a dictatorship can reach a state of being emotionally at one with its president, so directly affected by and near to him. The state's institutions had been destroyed, and could not save the people.

On a walk with Moses in his neighborhood one day, we stopped at an acquaintance's home as a courtesy. There, I witnessed a ceremony in which the family gathered around a photograph of the president hung on the wall, and prayed to him, wishing that he should be secure. Moses and I also clasped our hands. The president, his lips gently parted in the photograph, was seen as their sole protector.

Government spies were felt to be everywhere. And though on the streets people were as amicable and courteous, and making easy conversation, from its cities to its villages the country was tense, and waiting for some sign that the pressure might ease.

Newspapers expressed anger against the dissidents, anger against the journalists, anger against the enemies of the state who were trying to sabotage the president's success. The stories gained in extremity, and became personal attacks.

Perhaps more disturbing than the words was that they were treated as truth. Moses told me it was how the genocide had become so violent: journalists like him who had opposed the killing had been arrested, tortured, murdered. The people then bent over to show their support for the dictator. Words were no longer mere words: they became facts. The repression of words gave the genocide great force.

Now with the evident fear everywhere, the government's voice seemed to calm, and become somehow gentle, and coaxing. There were more and more references in the press to the country's "good citizens." Something insidious was being called upon in people's minds. It was the call of the Intore, the group to praise the president, which Cato had left our class to join.

The strange woman and the boy sat before me on wooden chairs in the government office. We were in the country's north, near the hills that led to a chain of volcanoes.

I had wanted to get out of the city, and had made a trip to see something the government was keen to show its citizens.

It had been a curiosity of mine to know if the dictatorship had its heroes, apart from the president. I had been directed to a certain people in this area.

The woman before me was elderly and frail. The boy next to her, not her son, was a strapping muscular figure. He observed me, and appeared unhappy. They were both from families that owned small potato and sorghum fields. They sat beside the district administrator, who had summoned them to speak to me as examples of the nation's citizen heroes.

The woman's son had been executed by the president's forces. He had been an *abacengezi,* part of a rebel group that had infiltrated these northern mountain villages and attacked the government's forces. Her son had hidden in her home for weeks at a time with rifles and rocket launchers, as did many sons during the rebellion. But on one of his visits this woman had denounced her son to the government. She told me this with pride.

I turned to the boy. He had been an *abacengezi* rebel. He too was denounced by his mother. But he said he was glad she had betrayed him, for it had shown him "the good way." The government had not killed this boy. It was felt something could be done with him. He had been sent to the *ingando,* the military-style training camp, and turned into a loyal supporter for the government.

These women—there are many who betrayed their sons to the authorities—do not hide from shame, or show any sense of difficulty about the choice they made. They in fact seek to be paraded, to meet the visitor, whom they asked to spread word of their accomplishment. It was the government's way of breaking society. These were its heroes: they set the example that even the bond between mother and child should not come before one's loyalty to the state.

"He deserved it," the woman told me of her dead son.

"Can you trust your mother now?" I said to the boy.

"Without her I would not have known how to love my country," he said, in a clear voice.

I had hoped for solidarity among the journalists in my class, but with this as the example—the regime exacted the maximum from its people—it was inevitable that they had betrayed one another. I imagined they must have felt lost. How to give yourself to an idea, when something as primal as your mother could betray?

There was only one father in this society.

And it seemed impossible in such a country for one to trust a friend, or a colleague, even a teacher. This was the ultimate goal of the Intore: total loyalty.

I watched the woman's lean face, her shifting eyes. She repeatedly professed happiness that she had helped to kill her son—he had been the enemy. Her smile was haunting, frightening. Something very deep seemed at work in her expression, in her countenance. I could not get her smile out of my mind.

The journalists brutally crippled, I felt we had perhaps to change direction, to step back and take stock, and try something different. Without doubt, we had to move more carefully.

Our program was also running out of funds. We would soon reach the end of our contractual period. This weighed on me considerably, and complicated the difficulty of finding a solution.

At this time, I worked nervously in the office. I worried constantly that we were being spied on, and that our organization would be shut down. The trip to the *abacengezi* had also stayed with me, with its sense of the possibility of betrayal.

It seemed natural that the authorities would come after us. But I tried to convince myself that they would not. We were too small. We had operated in the country for several years, conducting a variety of projects that did not directly confront the repression. Several senior government officials, even some close to the president, had once worked for our program.

I wondered if it would be enough to protect us.

Almost every prominent journalist we had trained had been touched—had either fled or been arrested. Jean-Léonard, just before joining us, had been killed. And the others had effectively been silenced by the spilling of his blood.

It gave me a chill to think of the clampdown. But there was little that I felt I could do. The only way for me to work was to train the journalists openly. Secrecy would have entailed even greater risk, and an entirely different operation.

And if our money ran out we might anyway have to leave.

I was more careful in locking up the office. We had a few computers, recorders and other equipment for the journalists that it would be a shame to lose. At the end of each day I made a round of the doors and windows. It was in fact a pointless exercise—we had employed a local security company, and our neighborhood was safe. Any theft would be a job of the government, and against that there was nothing I could do. Still, I made my rounds.

I also walked to the office on the pavement, at the far edge away from the road, always facing the traffic.

It was at around this time that I received a surprise visit. I was in the classroom, standing in the main hall beside a window, browsing through some recent newspapers spread over a table.

I had seen and heard of Roger a few times since our last meeting. Once was on national television. He had been speaking critically at a government conference, talking about the need for the rule of law in the country, and how the justice was dominated by the government.

I had thought about Roger as well, and wondered if that man following him had somehow harmed him. I had worried for the young journalist, but had hesitated to give him a call, partly out of a fear that his conversations were being listened to. I thought it was how the government so easily separated people, prevented them from coming together, even sharing thoughts.

Now Roger rushed into the office. He had not called beforehand. I asked, surprised at my own brusqueness, what he wanted.

He said something had happened, and that he needed to speak with me urgently.

I did not move. So he began to tell me.

He was being harassed by the government, and needed to get out of the country at once.

I took him into my private room and shut the door. I asked him to tell me what had happened, precisely. I was already worried someone might have heard.

He showed me samples of stories he had published—two reports on the military, and about the recent surge of mobilization and recruitment. The stories contained a number of spelling errors, but Roger seemed to have access to good sources.

I told him we should leave the office: someone might walk in on us talking, and I could not guarantee that these premises were not being watched. Roger suggested we speak in a neutral place. I took him to the yard of a nearby school.

We passed a police van on the way, with its soldiers sitting back to back in the open air, surveying the street. On the school's mud road we were approached by a group of teenage boys wielding batons. "Community police?" I asked. They were like the Intore. Groups of civilians were being formed and made to patrol the country, to root out the enemy. Roger tensed. But they passed without taking any interest in us.

I had walked by this school from time to time. A little sign was inside, with the word "Discipline." We now stood in the yard, which was empty but would soon fill with children, for it was almost the recess hour.

"When an anonymous number calls, I dread to pick it up," Roger said. "It's always the government informers, calling to threaten me."

He said his blog was flourishing. The number of readers had rapidly grown. The authorities had warned him to curb his reports, but he had not obeyed. "I am not afraid despite everything that has happened."

What about the propaganda job he had been offered?

"I couldn't do it," he said. "I couldn't do it. But I should have known that it would be more trouble when I refused that job."

I asked why he had approached me.

He said our training program had a good reputation. Even reporters who no longer practiced recommended it. And he was certain that we would be able to help him.

"But we don't evacuate journalists," I said. "You know that."

"My life is in danger. What do you want me to do."

"You need to find some help urgently."

"Well help me, I'm here." He seemed to be confused, as if he had not the slightest idea what he should do. I wondered if this too was an effect of the isolation. I wanted to help.

"How long has this been going on for?" I asked.

"Some weeks. Now things have become urgent."

I asked if he had sought any assistance. He replied that he had written to the Committee to Protect Journalists, in New York, but someone in the president's office had then shown him the application that he had filled out online. He didn't trust people abroad anymore.

And given the current situation—how the authorities were intensifying their surveillance—he didn't trust anyone in the country either.

"There are people who can help you," I said. "Have you tried the embassies?"

He said that if he sought refuge the embassies would simply hand him over to the government. They had done it already with a previous *Umuseso* editor—the Americans had refused to give him cover. The journalist had been forced to fend for himself.

Could his family not do something?

"My mother is old and lives alone on her farm. I don't have the heart to even tell her what is happening, she would be too worried."

I asked who was threatening him.

He said it was the Ministry of Defence, that he had been stopped on the street the previous week by men in a car. They had taken him to a secret detention center, where he had been held for a night. They had threatened to torture him. The experience had been harrowing.

When I asked if he didn't have friends in the military from his child soldier days he laughed strangely and mockingly, and this laugh seemed suddenly to reveal his fear. "They are too afraid even to come near me."

His case seemed serious, and already mature: there was nothing I could do if the Ministry of Defence was pursuing him. This army was legendary for its ruthlessness and efficiency. They would without hesitation kill anyone who got in the way of their work.

I explained my constraints. I told him I was not specialized in evacuating journalists in danger. My job was to train those who wanted to stay, who wanted to work to improve conditions here, who could eventually confront the system.

I stopped short of saying I had never before evacuated a journalist.

"Don't give up now," he told me. "I know a lot has happened recently."

I said that was not the reason for my refusal.

"We can still win."

I said nothing.

He became angry, and his voice turned into a squeal. It was sharp, almost as if he would begin to break down and cry.

"I've come to you as a final resort. The journalists in this country are being destroyed. You know this. You know we are being punished simply because we fight for freedom for our people. Some have lost their lives, others have fled. Now we are not so many. I know how these people think. I am capable." He sighed. "We have a responsibility to see this through. Right now I am asking for your help."

I said I would see.

But it wasn't enough for him. He said he was under pressure, and that he had to do something immediately.

He looked at me awhile, now silent. The twilight had arrived, and the angled rays of the sun turned the grass around us fluorescent.

Roger spoke. "Listen, not long ago in my country we had a genocide. People were killing one another with machetes and knives. Not hundreds of people, not thousands of people. Almost one million people. The world was watching us on TV. United Nations soldiers were here. All the foreigners were here. They watched us."

He paused.

"They did nothing."

The doors of the classrooms were beginning to open, and the first children were coming out.

"Now we are again in a time of need. Our brothers and sisters are being killed, tortured and taken to secret prisons. We are asking for help."

I was frozen in my place.

"Will you just stand again and do nothing?"

That evening I organized to get drinks with a group of genocide survivors. I had expected to find Moses there, but he was at the last minute unable to join us. I wanted some relief—the survivors were among the few who, when they wanted, spoke freely. We were about a dozen in all, coming and going from our table at the bar, in a noisy neighborhood near Moses' house. The group was fairly private about their survivor status, and as such I felt privileged that they had allowed me to come.

The conversation began easily: they exchanged notes on their families, told each other about the women they were seeing. One of them had traveled to India for a long-needed shoulder operation to treat a machete injury from the genocide, and the others had contributed money toward this. But then, triggered by a mention of the recent memorials, talk turned to the president.

"The genocide becomes a theater, like a circus, under this regime," one of them said.

History, particularly of the time of the genocide, was so vital to the president's repression that for many years it was not taught by schoolteachers but by soldiers. This history had now been implanted in the national school curriculum. The president, a survivor said, had known where people had been gathered to be massacred during the genocide. They had been in camps, churches, schoolyards. But after opposing the deployment of U.N. peacekeepers, the president had directed his troops away from these people and toward his military targets, so he could focus on the conquest of power. This happened repeatedly: tens of thousands of people were killed in these preventable massacres, though some managed to escape and survive. But in the years after the genocide the president had silenced the survivors so they could not say what they had seen. He had taken over survivors' associations by placing figures of his regime in key positions. The associations praised the president. With bright bulbs hanging over us, the survivors spoke of how the president "disdained" them. He insulted the survivors in private with phrases like "*your* genocide," though he too was Tutsi. "We tell the president that we are sensitive to such words, but he and his people keep using them." The president told survivors that they had not suffered, as he had, for years in exile. "He compares his childhood humiliation to the genocide. The regime, in the way it organizes the memorials, in the way that it speaks to us, negates what we experienced. It makes us feel ashamed that the genocide happened to us." As with Moses, the season of remembrance had stirred in the survivors such frustration. All they could do was speak among themselves.

I felt a small panic: the conversation had heightened my sense of disquiet. Roger's words had been affecting. And the genocide—its symbolism was powerful. Would I regret having turned him away? Would I remain a passive bystander to the violence? I felt he had appealed to me personally, that with his mere words I had been implicated. And at the same time something about him gave hope that the government brutality might be fought.

Another round of drinks was ordered. But some survivors got up to leave and were teased about their new women. These women were apparently naughty; the men complained loudly that the girls were too possessive. I had the impression that this was how the survivors got on with their lives.

I wanted to talk to Moses. He told me to meet him outside the city.

Traveling there, as I observed the countryside I thought often of the landscapes Gibson had crossed. He must have been in a terrible fright. But the place was too calm, too beautiful. I found it difficult to imagine his state of mind. And so I felt divorced from what I was seeing, and also from him.

The wind sounded in my ears, a fast, streaky wind. We were near the top of a hill, where I had gotten off the bus and was standing beside a friend Moses had sent.

Moses himself was not to be found. From our position we could see a deep valley patterned with paddies. Cut into the hill was a rising dirt road. And I thought I could hear a regular beating carried by the wind, like of metal on stone.

The friend of Moses started to walk toward the sound, along the red dirt road. He was carrying a sheaf of papers, and indicated that I should follow. I noticed, upon walking, that the hillside edge of the road was sharp and the gutters were neatly chiseled in—the road had been newly leveled.

It was the dry season in Rwanda, and dust was everywhere, thrown up into a red haze and reaching into one's body, into one's ears and nostrils.

We turned a corner, and there in front of us was the source of the noise: a group of about twenty or thirty men, wearing peasant clothes and jackets, and the cowboy-style leather hats of the local farmers.

But they were wielding shovels and machetes, and working on the road. I realized immediately to where I had been brought. These men were killers from the genocide, who had been commissioned for the *travail d'intérêt général,* or public works, as punishment for their crimes.

They were prisoners of the state, though they lived in open-air countryside camps. And though these were some of the most dangerous men in the country—convicted of some of the most heinous crimes known to humanity—there was hardly a guard in sight.

It was an indication of the level of control of the regime: where could these men run to? In a state where citizens sided with the government there was nowhere to hide. Even with minimal security the prisoners would not escape; they would obediently serve out their sentences.

Again, it was the word of authority that had sentenced them. Simple words had attained such power.

I was wary of following Moses' friend—suddenly the feeling of being amongst such men, wielding machetes, had a visceral reaction on me.

And I knew I should not be here. We were violating the government's orders.

But the friend, dressed in grey pants and a pinstriped shirt, like an ordinary Rwandan, moved between the men. Some turned to look, but most of them kept at their repetitive work, ignoring our presence. An official was among them, a young man in uniform. The friend walked up to him and said something, presumably to introduce us. The official nodded.

I hurried up to the friend and asked what he had said about us.

"Don't worry about it," he told me.

I realized that Moses had planned this, that he had used his contacts in government.

I saw an elderly, bulky man and was immediately attracted by his face. He was wearing an old leather sleeveless jacket and seemed to bear a kindly expression. I walked up to him and asked how he was. But he said nothing. I asked again, and he replied, in perfectly accented French, *"Je ne parle pas le français."* I don't speak French.

I followed him, watching his work, but the man moved away, and stood beside the young official. I understood that he was determined not to speak.

Everything was a surprise—my being here, my approaching them. I was proceeding more by instinct than by any calculation, and I became taut with anticipation, with the realization that I was among men who were exceptional.

Many of the killers had been released from prison by the government, partly because the prisons had been overcrowded. They lived on the hills, but were loath to be identified. It was usually only possible to talk to them with some authorization from the state. And in that case one was immediately compromised—for one did not know if they were talking to you or if they were acting out the part that the state had set for them, in the "theater" that Moses had talked about.

One had almost to be a stranger to have any hope of a sincere moment with an interlocutor in a dictatorship. The answers always depended on whom one was talking to; the dictatorship allowed for little notion of truth.

The killers of the genocide were like a secret, an ultimate secret, proof of the deepest emotions within the country, products of the most extensive manipulations and propaganda.

I was reminded of what Gibson had said to me about the lights. He had shown me that the dictatorship had made two worlds: one for visitors and another for the citizens. One in which the explosion was real, and another, in parallel, in which it was not. One in which there was memory, and another with new trauma. A world in which the streetlights seemed wonderful, signs of progress, and another in which they were frightening.

The killer, or *génocidaire,* was a sort of myth. In the visitor's world that Gibson had talked about they were the worst kind of citizen, responsible for the ill. They were the symbols of evil.

It was extremely difficult to meet these men, so fabled in this society and the history of humanity.

And here, I was alone, on an isolated hill, with the opportunity.

I felt I was crossing at that moment from one world into the other.

We passed the end of the group now. Moses' friend walked on, and I followed. The road curved around the hill in a wide arc. Before us were two men, in simple clothes, sitting on a rock. I stopped.

The friend pushed me forward. "Go now, this is your chance."

I walked ahead. The men put down their machetes.

I said I was a visitor to the country, and asked if they would like to talk. The men were both sweating, and both shook my hands, greeting me in French. They looked around—the supervisor was around the corner and could not see us. Without responding, they started to walk up the hill, farther from the working group, and now we were walking together.

I turned to look; the friend was no longer there. I grew nervous.

One of the men had a hat on with the flag of the president's party. He was younger than the other, who was in blue overalls. I asked what they had worked as before. The younger man said he used to run a little shop in the town of which the older man had been the *bourgmestre,* or mayor. The older man had also been a teacher.

"What did you teach?" I asked the older man.

"Civic education."

That he had been a *bourgmestre* meant that he had been quite senior in the killing operations. The *bourgmestres* would organize and plan the killing. They were the ones who received the orders from the state to carry out the genocide, and who were responsible at the local levels for the extermination.

The man seemed quite calm, however.

He didn't seem to want to ask me anything, or know anything about me.

I asked what he remembered of the genocide.

"It has been some years," he said. "And we were mad then. It is sometimes difficult to remember one's moments of madness."

"What did you think of it?"

"It was bad, wrong. The state let us down by ordering it."

"Why didn't you refuse?"

He scoffed.

I asked if my questions were disturbing them.

"On the contrary," he said, "we rarely get to talk to outsiders, and we are pleased to talk with you."

I asked what he, being a teacher, would have taught in the schools to have avoided the genocide.

"Human rights," he said unequivocally.

I thought it was propaganda, a practiced response, and I mentally dismissed it.

I asked why they were building the road.

He said it was punishment. And punishment was good, after what they had done.

"But it seems the state asked you to kill, and you killed. Now they ask to build a road, and you build a road."

The older man turned to the younger one, who had so far been silent: "Tell him, tell him! Tell him how it is."

But the former shopkeeper was silent.

The *bourgmestre* continued, "That's how it is! They tell us to make the road, we do it. They tell us to kill, we would do it. They ordered us to kill at seven a.m. We started as early as nine a.m. All we need is the order. And look there"—he pointed to the adjacent hill, at the top of which we could see a crowd, a platform, and many flags—"he tells us to come to sing for him, and we will go."

Indeed, it was to see the rally that Moses had proposed I join him. I figured he must be on that hill.

"Tell me what goes on in your mind. Tell me why if he tells you to go you must, or if he tells you to kill your friends or neighbors, you do that also—"

"Young man," he said, "maybe you didn't understand what I meant by human rights. What I mean is that in this kind of country we don't know where the state ends and where we begin." He made his hand come over his head, to show the looming state.

"And if I don't know where I begin, I am worth nothing, I don't have any rights. Then how to feel that another person has rights? How to respect that person. In this country we don't even know if we exist as people. We are not individuals, we are agents of the state."

Our footsteps on the dirt path made a crunching sound that was loud.

I wondered if languishing many years in prison had given him the chance to reflect. It was perhaps the most profound statement on the condition of freedom I had heard in the country, and it had come from a man who had deprived many hundreds, probably, of that most fundamental right—to life.

I felt he had passed me something precious.

We walked some more. I asked the younger one what kinds of things he had sold in his shop. "Small sachets of food," he said, "and detergent, and fruit."

He said he would like to reopen his shop when he was released from the prison camps, which should be in a few years. The *bourgmestre* said he would be too old when he returned to his village, and there would be nothing for him to do.

He was not sure if the state would want him for anything.

"It was a different time, the genocide," he said. "I will never forget that madness."

I asked if there was anything he regretted.

"The big politicians escaped," he said. "They told us to kill, but are now in five-star foreign prisons, with good food and televisions. We little people must bear the consequences for their decisions."

We had walked quite some way up the hill now. Suddenly remembering Moses' friend, I asked if I could take their leave, and I started to run down the hill as fast as I could.

I passed the group of working men, with their supervisor still watching over them, and the old man who had not answered my greetings. He saw me and averted his eyes.

And there I saw the friend, sitting on the grass, waiting for me. He didn't ask what I had done. "Moses is there," he said, pointing at the adjacent hill, which was filling with people.

The president was about to come.

•   •   •

We arrived by motorcycle, mine following his. Moses was at the back of the rally grounds, sitting on some concrete steps. On seeing me he slowly rose, and leaning on his cane made it down step by step.

The friend left us—perhaps to move elsewhere in the crowd.

"Did you get to talk to them?" Moses asked.

"I did."

"Good."

"Why did you send me?"

"These things are important."

Gibson had said on his last night that one had to seek out what the state did not show—and perhaps did not know it was showing—and that there it was possible to find truth.

"I have needed to ask you some advice," I said. "It's why I wanted to meet."

"About what?"

"This journalist called Roger." I gave him Roger's full name.

"Wait a little," he said. He had seemed to have had trouble hearing, and then to become distracted.

The crowd was growing in spurts, as large green buses, donated to the government by Japan, brought a hundred supporters in at once. There must have been more than a thousand people already.

The Intore were particularly active. Groups of thirty or forty men and women in T-shirts bearing the face of the president ran in circles and sang devotional songs to the president, urging everyone to sing with them. Some of the youths were mouthing the words, without joining the frenzied dancing. They had stickers of his image pasted onto their foreheads.

The Intore passed our section. But a middle-aged man started to dance, wildly, singing in praise of the president. He started to go from group to group, goading the girls and touching the boys to join him. He smiled pitifully. "Kagame the hero, the king who has descended from heaven. We love Kagame, vote for Kagame!" he screamed. "Aho! Aho!" But unlike with the Intore the youths distanced themselves from him.

"It is what dissent has become," Moses told me. "Things have gotten so bad that you have to act mad to show opposition." And apparently one dissented by excess praise. The youths recognized his insincerity, and so kept their distance.

"I feel sad to see these young people," Moses said. "They are all drunk. They have been fed Primus, like during the genocide." Primus was the local beer that the killing mobs had been plied with, and so it held some symbolism.

"The sad thing is that they don't know. They are told to come cheer, and given the drink as a bribe. I saw young people kill during the genocide. Primus was rare; most people drank banana wine. So the government gave them Primus and told them to kill. That's why these campaigns hurt, it hurts to see these young people receiving beer from the government."

We were in a large field—otherwise a football stadium—decorated extensively in the colors of the president's party. Red white and blue streamers hung from poles. Flags were draped over the main stage in front of us.

I heard a voice from behind—"Why are you taking notes?"

I stopped writing in my little pad. It was a policeman, in dark blue uniform.

"Are you a journalist?" he asked.

The accusation was grave.

"No," I lied. "I'm just a visitor passing through, and I came here because I want to see the president. Are journalists not allowed here?"

I spoke in English, the language of the country's elite, though Moses and I spoke in French, which was used by the masses. It seemed to help my case.

"I have seen you," the policeman said. "Looking and writing, looking and writing." He raised and lowered his head to imitate my movements. I became worried, that we had been noticed, observed.

"Was it wrong to?"

"You can't look and write," he said. "It is not allowed. If you want to know something you ask him"—he pointed at Moses. "We know him, and we can find him if he tells you some lies. But you are not allowed to look and write by yourself."

I asked what would happen.

"Listen," the policeman said in a lower voice. "I am in uniform, but there are many people here who are not, who are observing you."

"Secret service?"

"Just do it"—he clenched his teeth, still smiling—"I am saying it for your own good." He said a few words to Moses, I imagined to indicate that he was responsible for me, then nodded and left, to stand some distance behind us, beyond a row of youths at the back of the crowd.

I put the pad in my pocket.

Moses said, "Secret service."

I looked at him questioningly.

"The police are always brutal. Because they have no power, they just follow the orders. You saw how nice this man was being with you? He has power."

I had noticed that he spoke fluent French and English.

"Yes, he was well educated," Moses said. "He spoke to me in High Kinyarwanda." It was a form of the Rwandan language associated with the monarchy.

I asked what the problem had been with my taking notes.

"We have an oral culture," he said. "People get nervous when you write. Writing also leaves proof. If you don't write notes the world can be made different. People's memories can always be questioned, molded."

One could not look and write. The narrative was so controlled—even what one saw with one's eyes. It was again the two worlds Gibson had shown me. One had to see the lights as progress; one wasn't allowed to ask why the people did not use those roads. One had to see the world as the dictatorship described it. To look and think for yourself was to dissent.

It was a remarkable insight into the method of the government that this policeman had revealed.

I looked around, and wondered what the people were seeing. How did they look at this stadium, the ceremony, the president? How had the world been shaped for them? I thought of what the *bourgmestre* had said about the nature of the killing, how it had seemed to them.

There was a rumble of cars—jeeps with sirens appeared, seeming to clear the way and scouting for threats. After a while a sleek black car with dark windows swerved into an area nearby. The crowd surged, and we lost sight of it.

I started to write on the palm of my hand—which became covered in ink over the course of the rally. I held the hand in a fist to hide what had been written.

The Intore incited the crowd. Still in the car, he allowed the cheering and singing to continue. I spotted, among the presidential coterie that had emerged, Cato, wearing a brown suit and a bulging yellow tie. He seemed in awe of his place, beside the president. I was not surprised—he had been a skilled journalist, and had a sharp mind. A television crew had also arrived.

In one corner was the Intore chief—a burly man, he epitomized the nature of the organization, the betrayal inherent in it. For he had once been a high official in the previous regime, which had fought a war with the president. And now he was in charge of inculcating devotion for the president in the country's youth. There was a ruthlessness to the president's campaigns; it required a betrayal of oneself.

But there was something else in this scene of more than a thousand people cheering, waving their flags, chanting for the president. It was a show to all his opponents, a show of how much he could control, and the force with which he ruled the country.

He at last revealed himself.

The gaunt figure ascended the stage. It was the first time I was before him. And I felt awed. The man who looked so weak and frail could control so much, could mobilize so many people behind him. There was an aura of power around his figure, a sense of invulnerability. He moved with ease on the stage. It was the aura of a president whose power was absolute.

One sensed the minds and spirits of the people had somehow become attuned to him, were somehow connected with his limp smile, with the slight movements of his body.

I thought of the journalists trying to combat his regime, and felt, in the midst of this rally, what was before them. A tension rapidly grew within me. The rally—the people cheering, I could hear nothing else, and the jumping and singing crowds jostled me—was to feel viscerally the government's power.

It was a show of force intended for a certain audience: for anyone who thought of opposing him—for anyone who thought disobediently.

The president started to dance awkwardly on the stage, shaking elbows and knees to the music, but out of rhythm. People from the villages were brought onstage to begin the praise. A woman said she had started with one cow and now owned a farm, and that everyone could be like her; they should thank the president. A child was ushered up and read a poem about how the president had ended the genocide and saved them. A man spoke about the prosperity of the country since the president had come to power, and how proud the people were of the tall buildings in the capital as well as the reduction of poverty in the countryside—all products of the vision of their enlightened leader. He exhorted the people to be loyal to this leader, for all good things would come from him.

Everyone was waiting anxiously for his words.

It was also a show of force because the rally was unnecessary.

The president's election opponents had all been neutralized. Victoire, the woman accused of being a criminal in the papers, had been barred from registering as a presidential candidate and even from leaving the capital. Her private secretary had been charged with participating in the genocide, which he first denied, and then strangely confessed to, probably hoping for leniency. A young politician had been imprisoned on charges of criticizing the government's policies—which was not allowed even during elections. Several members of opposing political parties had been beaten up by the police. And not long ago a political opponent, once a member of the president's own party, was found almost beheaded, his body mutilated.

Everything had been done to ensure the president was unchallenged.

But still he organized these massive rallies—a dozen of them in every corner of the country.

And more and more the people urged the others to show devotion, show loyalty to the supreme leader.

The president was now benevolent. He had left the killing to his courtiers, as Agnès had written. Once the public displays of allegiance were over he told the people that all this was their achievement.

He came up to the standing microphone and said Rwanda was a democracy. This democracy had been instituted by the people, he said, not by him. It had been instituted not because foreigners had demanded it, but because the people of Rwanda wanted to construct their own future. So those who criticized the government were in fact insulting the Rwandan people and what they had built. The critics were looking down on the miraculous progress an African people had made to recover from a genocide. He said it was why he had built institutions that were independent and democratic, and that served all the people. The country had moved away from the divisive politics and repression of previous regimes. He urged the people to always strive to do better, and to work to further the nation on its current path of progress.

I wondered if he might believe what he was saying. Perhaps he believed in his goodness, and in his descriptions of a free country. The conviction and clarity and the lack of hesitation with which he spoke gave the impression of a divine kind of confidence. And even as he spoke his forces were carrying out more acts of repression, and were subjugating the people.

But they cheered raucously here, each trying to outdo the other in the way that he or she danced. A villager had built from scraps a little wooden car painted in the colors of the president's party. His friends were trying to get him to the front of the crowd so that he might show this object of his devotion to the leader.

I quivered in my place, feeling what was approaching those who wanted freedom. This was the power they were working against—not just him, but all those who had submitted and pledged allegiance. It was the purpose of his show.

This was a man whose forces had overseen so many killings, arrests, disappearances, so many cases of torture. Normally invisible, his power was brought alive.

I turned to Moses. "What do you think about Roger? He's asking for our help."

"What happened to him?"

"He has a news website that reports a fair amount on the army. Some of his reports displeased the government."

"Roger used to be in the army," Moses said.

"Yes, he told me."

"He did?"

"What do you think we should do for him?"

Moses seemed to reflect. "He's a small guy," he said. "Very small. He won't get anywhere."

"He seems one of the few who are still unafraid."

"Did you ask if he knows me?"

"He said he did, but vaguely."

"Shouldn't that tell you something about how serious he is? All the serious journalists know me very well."

I wondered if it was Moses' conceit showing.

"He's a small guy," Moses repeated. "Don't bother, don't waste your time."

I noticed something from the president's speech—how he had derided all the country's leaders who had come before him. And I wondered if this was also part of the repression, to allow the people no ideals, to tarnish everyone they had looked up to in the past. The new ideals of the country had been instituted— they were the president, the *abacengezi* mother and those who expressed total loyalty. I remembered the mother's smile.

I sought out Roger the moment I returned to Kigali, wondering if something might have happened to him. But I was unable to reach the journalist for several days, and began to worry for his safety. Had I come too late?

And when I eventually did make contact, it turned out my intuition had been well-founded—he had indeed been harassed by the authorities. The men had begun to make good on their threats. They had come again, picked him off the street, and started to beat him at a secret detention center. He showed me the bruises on his wrists.

The blood had clotted where the veins had been constricted by the pressure. I touched the blue skin. It was soft from the swelling. I felt pity for him.

But Roger said he could not stop what had been begun. "I have had enough. Enough of waiting for the day I will be free. I want it now." He had decided, he said, despite his troubles, to try to penetrate the government.

"I thought about what you said the last time," he said. "What good would I be outside the country? I should do what I can while I'm still here. I don't want to leave."

"That was not what I intended," I told him. "I just said I could not help you get out."

He said he was trying to cultivate a source in the president's office. I was surprised. I asked him how. He said a senior officer might agree to become an informant. Roger's idea was to infiltrate the president's inner circle and discover his plans for after the election. He had heard, for example, that a secret contraception campaign had begun, targeting poor women from communities known to silently oppose the president's rule. Men from those groups had already been arrested. What other major policies would affect the people? Who would he target next to cement his power?

I asked who was conducting the secret contraceptions. Roger said government doctors, under the guise of public health programs. The doctors' training was being funded by Western countries, which the government furnished with statistics to show how much good was being achieved. Testimonies were regularly collected from the population to show it was happy with the programs. Sometimes the Western officials visited the field, and the people themselves told them how happy they were.

Roger had also heard that men were being enlisted in the army. What for? The army had too many soldiers as it was, and he said it was strange that they were looking for new recruits. Unless a military excursion, or a war, was being planned.

"The president is getting rid of the journalists for a reason," Roger said, pensively. "He is thinking into the future, of eradicating dissidence not only in his opponents but also in their children. He has a plan in mind, starting with this election, to keep power with his close ones for many generations. This is what is at stake at this moment. This is why we have to act."

I asked why he did not seem afraid.

He said, "I constantly have to block out the fear. Listen, I think my future has already been decided. It is in some official's mind, or in a folder on a table in the president's office. That is our reality in such a country—our lives are determined by other men, not by God. That is the power of this government."

And here was someone, I thought, who was not going to give in, to heed the call of the Intore. Roger had changed his mind, decided to stay in the country, and counter the government. I admired his resolve, with which I felt he might be able to achieve something.

That evening we went on a walk. It was dark, and Roger took me to a crossroad near the Ministry of Defence. The area was brightly lit, with the ministry sitting atop a resplendent gardened hill. "You know what's under here?" Roger said, pointing at the garden. It was a military warehouse, in the center of the city, beneath this deceptive cover of flowering plants. He said it was to defend the government against a coup, though officially it was meant to protect the population.

The government had used armored personnel carriers from the warehouse once, not long after the genocide, Roger said. Some students were protesting the lack of access to university posts, and the government had gunned down the protesters.

"After that, it's very difficult for the people to come out and speak their mind. People remember these events. Have you noticed we don't have demonstrations in the country?"

There was in fact no life on the city's streets. It had not always been like this—once musicians had lined the pavements playing improvised tunes and hawkers had spread out plastic sheets with their wares: eggs, soda, clothes, cigarettes. Such were the streets of every neighboring country. But the Rwandan government had banned the hawkers and musicians from a fear that through street music people would pass on subversive messages and organize dissent. It was another way of preventing people from communicating, from associating and sharing ideas.

And walking down these streets—which so many visitors lauded for their cleanliness and tranquility—one felt the isolation that had been imposed on the people. Only the government was present.

A sound above, and the police helicopter passed, its harsh spotlight moving over the neighborhoods. Roger looked up, straining to see. He seemed so innocent.

The helicopter moved away.

Roger twitched nervously. As we walked in the ministry's garden he pointed below us and said that tanks had recently been given to Rwanda by the American government—Abrams tanks, high-performance machines that made the president feel secure.

The world, he said, wanted the Rwandan president to stay a long time. And this was also what the journalists faced: not only the government, but also its allies, who made it so powerful.

His phone started to ring. He looked at the screen and answered it, and began to talk in Kinyarwanda to a succession of people. He kept his voice low, betraying no emotion until after the callers had hung up and Roger was left saying, "*Umva, umva!*"—Listen, listen!

The callers were summoning Roger to the Ministry of Defence. They had somehow received word that he had been making contact with politicians and former soldiers. It had raised suspicions.

"Did you perhaps tell someone about me?" he asked, looking straight at me.

I said that I was not so thoughtless as to do such a thing.

He seemed perplexed; he felt someone had betrayed him. But who could it be?

A dinky little car passed us on the road—"Policemen," Roger said, with some distaste. "They always use these dirty vehicles to pick up people."

We walked shoulder to shoulder, the two of us alone on the new road under the bright orange lights. But we no longer felt alone.

At dinner—we ate at his run-down hotel—Roger ordered a plate of fries. He said that even his sister could have been recruited by the authorities. He was beginning to trust no one. He said, under his breath, that he was beginning to feel isolated, and that the continual paranoia—the nervousness as the vote approached—was starting to take its effect.

"I know," he said to me suddenly.

"What?"

"I know about your friend, and how he had to leave."

Gibson?

He nodded at me. "I know. Don't worry, your secret is safe with me." He gripped his chest over the heart. "I'll keep it safe. I know you care about him."

"How did you find out?"

"I've been keeping track of these acts by the government."

My apprehension dropped away, and I felt glad that Roger was aware. I said, "He was a good man."

"A talented journalist, who didn't deserve what they did to him. I think about him sometimes, and also the other journalists who fled."

The shared secret, I felt, brought us closer. Perhaps it was because I no longer felt alone when I now remembered Gibson.

Roger told me not to touch the mayonnaise. He said fatty substances made ideal repositories for poisons. So we ate our fries dry and washed them down with soda.

Two of the older journalists from my class approached me in the office and requested that I help them cover the election. They said they came on behalf of the entire class, which had decided as a group that it wanted to report.

"We have learned a lot here," one of them said. "We would like to please continue to have your guidance and perspectives at this time."

Their names were Theo and Adolphe. And they expressed concern about recent developments, just days before the vote.

"When people are saying that the sight of soldiers on the street reassures them," Theo told me, "and a minister is informing hungry farmers how to dispose of their surplus grain, you know the problems are serious."

"People are saying that they will vote for the president because he has given them freedom." Adolphe sounded distraught.

"The election commission is saying it wants a one hundred percent turnout."

The following morning I sat in my office, thinking about what they had said, and pondering how to help them. It was early, and still dark. I felt in a sort of cocoon, ensconced in another body, as if I were going to be born, waiting to be delivered. A rooster was crowing, sensing the day.

After meeting Roger, I had felt what was happening to him was an indication for our journalists. Nothing good was about to come. But these students nevertheless wanted to hunt for news.

I felt infected by their spirit. Confined in the classroom, I was strangely able to think; when free one seemed somehow captive. I thought of the former killers working on the road: they were not free but had seemed so in their minds. And the people on the streets were supposed to be free but were not.

The rooster's crowing had become relentless, disturbing, and on an impulse I thought I would tie up its beak. But before I rose from my chair I realized that if I shut its beak the rooster could not nourish itself.

In my cocoon I became aware of my bodily sensations, of my breathing, of the blood pulsing in my veins. I felt enervated, that my body had no limit and had merged with the darkness.

We heard that journalists abroad were also attempting something difficult. A few former *Umuseso* reporters were trying to send copies of a clandestine newspaper into Rwanda.

The government official wore an exaggerated smile when I entered his office. He was a longtime politician who had occupied a string of senior government positions. For the past several years he and his party had officially collaborated with the president to rule the country. And he was one of three candidates the president had allowed to compete against him in the election.

The president wanted the appearance of a fair vote, with each party conducting its own campaign and four choices on the ballot. This man had acquiesced to the president's order to stand as a candidate in this theater.

To the extent that at one of his party's rallies, the chief organizer wore a T-shirt showing an image not of this man but of the president. She declared publicly that she would vote for the president. And she openly admitted that the president's party had financed this rally for his opponent—whose party hardly had funds.

I found the presidential candidate in a high-backed chair surrounded by warmly colored wood-inlaid walls.

Though I was interviewing the candidate, I was unsure if I should publish reports on the election. I feared they would draw unnecessary interest to our program, and possibly present a risk to my students and to myself.

We made some initial small talk: I asked how his campaign was proceeding. He was relaxed, easygoing as he told me about his party's program.

It was part of the candidates' theater to talk to journalists during the election campaign season.

I asked if he would criticize the president on any policies.

He started to tell me about the virtues of his party's program.

I interrupted him. "But will you criticize the president?"

He said, with some hesitation, "We don't see the necessity in criticizing the president."

"But he is your opponent."

"Yes, yes."

"I read your recent interview, in which you insist that you will win. Don't you want people to believe that the president has made any mistakes? Why should they vote for you?"

He raised his eyebrows. "It is difficult to criticize the president."

I told him that his election platform involved several advanced ideas: adjustments for market regulators, reform in government procurement, family planning, deficit reduction, and the privatization of education. It almost seemed like an American party's program.

He seemed proud.

"What about freedom?"

He seemed surprised.

"Your plan would be great in a country with freedom. In fact, reading your plan you would think that technocratic issues are the country's only problems, and that the people are free."

He said nothing.

"Why do you do it?" I asked, more quietly.

"What?" he said, suddenly attentive.

I mentioned some of the recent repression. "Why do you participate in this sort of government?"

He was quiet.

But I felt he was engaging me despite his silence—perhaps he wanted to talk, for at that moment he could have asked me to leave.

"Are you content living in this society?" I asked.

"Yes of course, my children are here."

"But many others have had to flee," I said, wistfully. "People with more beautiful offices, bigger houses and cars, who were once very close to the president, have had to flee their country. Why?"

"There isn't a plan for how to rebuild a country after genocide," he said, repeating the president's discourse. "In such circumstances it is normal that politicians have diverging opinions. This is not new in politics."

"But is it normal that they flee?"

He looked me in the eye. "I am following it closely," he said. "I am also worried. Do you think they were chased?"

"Why does divergence of opinion lead to insecurity for these people?"

"I don't know," he said. "It is a question I have asked myself."

He seemed sincere.

"Do people here have the courage to diverge with the power?" I asked.

He paused for a long time. Then suddenly he said, "Yes. The proof is us."

I wanted to laugh—but I didn't, because he spoke with such solemnity. He was telling me that this was the extent to which dissent was tolerated. One could go only as far as he and the candidates had in this election—and that was a chilling prospect.

He was telling me that his public theater was an act of courage.

But he had spoken to me, had revealed this much. And I felt that those in government who knew what was being done to their country and did not agree, were themselves powerless against the president's machine. They wanted badly to speak—even to a stranger.

He wiped his forehead with a handkerchief and smiled at me.

Showing me to the door, he said, "You ask a lot of questions." I could tell that he was indicating I should be more discreet

•   •   •

The president became even more pervasive. His image was on key chains, rearview mirrors and hats. Wartime mottos from his rebellion days were broadcast on the radio, eliciting familiar emotions. School-age children ran down streets and sang traditional songs that replaced "Jesus" with "Kagame." Everywhere one felt watched by these devoted, and that one's entire being—actions, thoughts and soul—were scrutinized. I felt profoundly unsafe for not being among the believers.

And as though reminding me of what awaited those who confronted the government, Gibson called. I could hardly believe it was him when I answered the phone—I recognized the voice at once. He shouted out his name as though I would not know—"It's me! Gibson!" I told him to be quiet, that it was dangerous. He did not repeat the error. We were both elated at being able to speak again. I could hear the joy in his voice.

But this quickly gave way to the pain of his current situation. "I am living in the slums," he said. "There is less likelihood that the government will find me here."

I asked if he had made any friends.

"I just got robbed," he said. He had not wanted to tell me immediately. I sensed his shame. "They took everything."

His little suitcase, which had contained the Virgin Mary, the money I had given him and a small camera I had lent him so he could continue his work as a reporter had been stolen.

"How did that happen?" I asked.

"I was in the communal shower," he said. "I don't know. But they knew where to come. I think they had been watching me."

Had he been detected? I felt some annoyance. I had given him that camera so he would be able to survive. I had imagined that he would have little support in the new place, have few people he could trust, would be vulnerable.

"I am sorry, I am sorry," he repeated. "I was stupid."

"Don't worry," I said. "It'll be fine."

"It was my fault," he said. "I don't know what to do. How will I carry on? I have no money. And I can't return home. I don't know. Should I just give up?"

"We will find a way, Gibson."

"I am sorry for everything that has happened." His voice was again full of shame.

I remembered how he had been before he had left. How he had agonized as he was forced out of his country. And now he moved with nowhere in mind, only out of a fear of being caught. I thought of all the ideas the young journalist had come up with, of the magazine that he had wanted to start, of his talent, of the hospital story by which one night I had discovered him and the prize he had won in the class. I felt sadness.

"I may have to return to Rwanda."

"You can't come. It's too dangerous," I said.

"I have no money left. I can't afford to stay in Uganda. I'm finished as a journalist. I will stop writing. If I do that, maybe my family will shelter me."

I asked if he might find a job.

Gibson said he had tried. He had contacted a local association of street hawkers, which was helping him obtain a streetside mat so he too could sell goods such as plastic key chains and cheap toys. He sounded dejected—this was not the work we had hoped for. It was only a step up from menial labor.

We hung up on that note. I started to make a list of international organizations that might be able to assist him.

Gibson also offered a vision of what might await my students, now. The fervor with which people had rallied around the president had made it a dangerous time. Many deep, almost religious feelings had activated the people. The cracks closed up. The clandestine newspaper of the *Umuseso* journalists, called *The Newsline,* was discovered in a bus arriving from Uganda. The mass of words on stacks of paper had alerted the border officials. The papers were confiscated. It was another defeat for those hoping to speak their minds, who were trying to pierce the propaganda; and it showed the futility of efforts from abroad. I turned to the class. I had assembled a small fund to allow the students to travel, as they were too poor to report on their own. I hoped this might encourage them. The fund represented a significant amount of money for us—five hundred dollars between them, for their transport, phone calls, food and reporting. The program was not left with much more.

It was all that was in our power. The students stayed in late after class those last few days, surmounting the problems of poverty in their homes and ignoring phone calls from family members who needed money and food, assistance, to write furiously, and discuss what could be done.

Two days before the vote they came in to pick up their sums. They were stiff, nervous, but optimistic. We gave one another tender high fives. I whispered some words of encouragement. And I watched them step out of the office one by one, full of determination and hope.

On the morning of the election I woke up early and walked down the hill on which my house was set, past many small bars, all quiet. I saw a number of people, with serious faces, walking downhill to cast their ballots; and some who were returning, who looked relieved.

The nearest polling station was at a neighborhood school, a long low building set in an open field. Before a row of classroom doors, ajar, were lines of people. They looked away. They did not want to talk with me: there seemed some sort of malaise.

Others were very open, and spoke loudly, in support of the president. An official made me write down my name—"Today we are very happy to see you."

He read my expression of surprise.

"It is good to receive visitors. I think you have seen the good behaviors of our people. The voters are getting started."

I noticed an official had been placed at every door to usher the people in. I went up and asked one for identity papers. Imagining that I was an official observer, he showed them to me—he was a member of the president's party. Those at the other doors were less naïve; they said they were electoral volunteers and asked who I was.

It was all the government needed to do: the eye of the president's party was upon the people. These volunteers were discreet, but the people had certainly noticed. And now one could construct the most private voting booth—completely closed, dark, empty, without windows; but still the people would believe they were observed.

I asked one of the voters about the men at the doors.

"They are electoral agents," he said.

I told him they were from the president's party.

"Oh?" he said, as if he did not know. But he quickly added, "It's not a problem; they don't exercise any influence on people."

The voting booths did not stock pens, or any marking tools. Because of illiteracy in the country, the government had ordered that people mark their ballots with thumbprints. In another place it might have been a reasonable solution; but these people who pressed their thumbs in the ink and then on ballots knew that their votes could now be traced.

There was no privacy in their imaginations for how the government would use all these thumbprints.

Members of the president's party were recruited as "electoral observers": they sat at the back of the voting rooms, silent, merely watching. It was again the exploitation of the language of democracy—to an outsider this person would be a perfectly legal presence, foreseen in the electoral rules. In Rwanda, these illiterate peasants wearing the president's face on their shirts took on an entirely different meaning.

Later that morning I went to the polling station where the president was to arrive. It was decorated in colorful streamers as though for a birthday. And I realized why I had hardly seen a Rwandan journalist at the other venues. They had flocked to be in the president's presence, and to report on His Excellency's vote. Under a specially set up tent they milled about in their best clothing, having been handed complimentary drinks. Meanwhile the rest of the nation went hardly reported. I was stunned to see, among these journalists, my students. They were not on their assignments, but greeted me with cheers as though I were an old friend. I felt awkward. I saw Theo, who had served as a leader, and asked him, "What about your reporting from the countryside?" He smiled. "I checked, and everything there is all right." He patted me on the arm. There was festive music around us; it was like at a party. I found out that another of our students had been arrested after hesitating to write up a piece of propaganda. But his arrest had not been for journalistic reasons. A colleague had accused him of harboring genocidal ideas. He was trying to put together proof against the allegation. People were beginning to be told what they thought, and were unable to speak, to combat these ideas imputed to them. It was altogether less violent and less confrontational now than when Jean-Léonard had been shot. The transition was smoother, calmer and less perceptible.

Journalism in the country seemed dead. One noticed this around the election.

A boy suddenly ran outside the polling station, calling out that the president's party was already planning a victory celebration.

The election was a masterpiece of authority. The vote passed in an ambience of total serenity. No negative incidents were reported in the country: there were no protests, no complaints, no boycotts or demonstrations. The people queued up obediently. None of the opposing candidates claimed procedural irregularities. They were playing the theater to perfection, and vowed they would accept the election's results.

I called the presidential candidate I had met before the vote. He said the latest polls had been disappointing; but he claimed to be still hopeful for a win.

The president indicated he would wait for the official results before making any pronouncements.

The country was teeming with visitors: foreign dignitaries, journalists, election observers. Reports from that day would be broadcast across the world. A careful decorum had to be maintained.

The official observers were unanimous in their praise. The African Union and the Commonwealth lauded the government's impeccable planning: how the booths had opened on time, how people had voluntarily lined up with their identity cards in the early morning, and how by 10:00 a.m. practically every citizen—the government claimed a 95 percent participation rate—had cast their ballot. By noon already the booths were empty.

"The world has important lessons to learn from Rwanda," gushed a European Union official. Embassy observers hailed it as the most orderly vote they had witnessed in their careers.

The immense order of the ritual inspired awe.

The young Spanish woman, caressing her long hair, introduced herself to me as a propagandist. Her job was to write up positive stories, in supplements to British newspapers, about governments seeking to improve their image on the world stage or seeking to attract foreign investment.

But she had found no business in Rwanda, because the foreign press was already so positive. "Journalists come to our country all the time," a senior minister had told her. "And are stunned by how well we run it."

The minister had shown her examples of such stories in eminent foreign publications. These were stories about the roads, the economic growth statistics, and how survivors of the genocide supported the president, with no mention of his forces' massacres or his repression.

Even the professional propagandist, who had worked in a dozen dictatorships before, was astonished.

At the counting of the votes that evening I stood in a booth and watched the officials read: "Kagame Paul," which later became "Kagame" and finally "Paul, Paul, Paul," which was shorter, easier to say. Some of the girls marking tallies on the blackboard began to laugh. They seemed themselves astonished at the extent of the control.

I said to one of these girls—"The people are obedient."

She nodded. "Yes, very obedient." She was still smiling.

"The president is strong today."

"Very strong."

"What if someone disobeys him?"

"He will ask for forgiveness."

A few of the ballots were improperly marked, and as though I was some guarantor of fairness the officials held a ballot up to me and asked: "Paul?" I nodded, and did not resist. I felt it was futile to resist against such force.

But later I would hear that in the provinces some had dared to dissent, that in parts of the country—known for having resisted orders to kill during the genocide—only 10 percent of the people had voted for the president. The mayors in those areas had panicked, worried they would lose their positions, and ensured that the ballots were altered. Now the question was whether they could make sure no one would pass on the truth to the president. The source of this information was someone in the election commission.

The results were exactly as Moses had predicted a month before. He had told me that it had been decided: the president would receive 93 percent, the next candidate 5 percent, and the remainder split between the others. The Intore were summoned and put on a gigantic celebration in the stadium. Thousands attended. More Intore made the rounds in each neighborhood. In the dark valley below my house I heard the screams—raw, brutal—until almost dawn.

If some websites and stories even slightly criticized the election, the Intore immediately logged comments ridiculing and denouncing the authors, and saying that they lived in Rwanda and were happy. They wrote vehement letters to newspapers defending the president and his victory—and always gave their full names, so they could be seen for this loyalty. They knew the president's office was watching.

The oppression was obvious to those with experience. A Russian U.N. worker I met three days after he arrived, when I asked what he thought of the country, said at once that it reminded him of the Soviet Union. He had noticed the tone of the newspapers. Another woman I met had grown up in Yugoslavia, under the dictator Tito, and just moved here. She had not known about the nature of the government—the international press was so positive. But after meeting some government officials she came home, sat down her British husband, and said to him: "You have to be very careful what you say in this country." Her husband had been oblivious. She told me it had been the way people spoke, their mannerisms, something about it all; she could sense the repression.

And having grown up in a dictatorship myself, in Dubai, I knew all too well what signs she was referring to; it was sometimes intangible; one felt it, but it caused a kind of terror; one felt weak.

By the end of the election the old guard of news journalists had been done away with: killed, imprisoned, exiled or, by fear, converted into Intore. There was a surge of youngsters who took their positions; we also started to get them in our class.

A number of them were the children of reporters once immensely respected in the country—for having dared to speak out during the genocide or having survived imprisonment and torture by the previous government. Some of their parents had been killed for confronting the repression.

I recognized some of these young journalists from the president's polling station. They were the new superstars. Rising to prominence easily, many had been offered jobs at popular radio stations. They were sent by their editors to gain skills at our program. But they were difficult to teach: they did not want to listen, talked incessantly about themselves and their families, and they demanded respect from their interviewees. The talent and intellect were not there, but without even the spirit of the journalist there was little that could be done.

I felt we were wasting our time in the program. But Moses said that he would try to find more deserving students. I felt sad for him, and thought he was unable to or did not want to see the truth of our situation—that we were sinking.

There was also the growing problem of money. With the dates approaching for the termination of our grants, we started to slow down the program, and think of ways to scale back. It seemed senseless to waste precious funds on undeserving students. I preferred to be dormant for a while.

Moses said it would be a travesty if we ran out of money and had to close.

And then Moses was sent for by the president's office. It happened while he was at the hospital, receiving treatment. His leg had started to hurt again—the leg the security services had tortured for hours by beating the sole of his foot with a wooden baton; it had permanently weakened his bones, and he had started to take repeated absences from the program because of it. The bureaucrats working for the president told him to report the next day, and gave him no reason.

From morning at the office we waited impatiently for news. The presidency was the central node of power in the country, the seat of almost every command that was sent out to the people. Like a fortress, hidden by trees, only the most powerful people entered its compound. It wasn't without reason that they called in someone, particularly an elderly man. We feared the worst.

But Moses returned. He was shaken. It wasn't what we had imagined—he had not been threatened or beaten. An aide to the president had asked him to fill out a lengthy form with his family history. They were going to recruit Moses as a spy.

He was to be deployed against his family, some of whom had fled the country and were intellectuals in the Rwandan communities in Europe and America. His task would be to befriend these aunts, uncles, cousins and nephews, and report on them to the government services.

It was possible that the authorities had caught on to his activities at our program. Sending dissidents for work abroad was a way to neutralize them. The same had happened to General Kayumba, who had been made the ambassador to India. But here they were inflicting a double punishment on Moses by asking him to turn on those who trusted him.

I had never seen the man in such a state. The leg still pained intensely—the nerves were almost burning, he said—and he would make his way from one chair to another, clutching his calf, and the armrests.

"I'm not sure," he told me in a moment of respite. "If you take these jobs you are damned. They use you and then dispose of you. But if you don't take the job you are damned. They see you as disloyal to the president."

I sent Moses home in a taxi—Claude, the driver who sometimes offered us a free lift, was not far and came at once—so he could rest. He was moaning in the car. He would have to find some way out of his predicament.

I met Roger, this time on the office premises. But we were in the garden, away from the main building.

The white flowers on the guava tree were beginning to turn into fruit—tiny green bud-like structures, many dozens of them on a single stalk, covering it like pimples. The tree reminded me of Gibson.

Roger said that the ministry officials were trying to talk him out of his reporting. But he had challenged them to take him to court.

"They tell me the law is only for use on their enemies," he said. "They want us to reach an amicable settlement. How can I do that? I have to insist on the law, so that any favor they grant me becomes a right for all our citizens. But they want to separate and isolate us, so we depend on them for favors, for our lives and for our freedom."

The grenade attacks had continued. There was still no proof of who was responsible for the blasts. Roger said that the army had recently taken Kayumba's brother, immobilized him, and placed him at one of the likely sites of a bombing. They had told him, "Tonight you will die because of your brother."

I wanted to check on Gibson, after our last conversation. He had returned to Rwanda and was living with his family, who did not want him at home, for fear that the government might come after them all. Gibson had stopped writing entirely. It was too dangerous; he felt it was better that he keep a low profile and stay at home as much as he could. We agreed that it was dangerous for us to meet. I felt artificially separated from him, that he was close by but painfully distant. He said he was going to turn to the family fields and work as a farmer. After this, he started a strange kind of communication with me. My phone would ring once but he would cut the line so it sounded like a beep. On the first occasion I immediately returned his call, but he did not answer. I grew worried.

The following evening he beeped me again. And these squeals of the telephone every couple of evenings, before I went to bed, became somehow reassuring. I would recognize his number and feel pleased. They became little signals of affection, a way for Gibson to communicate that he was surviving.

I began to wait expectantly for these beeps from the young journalist who had renounced his work.

Roger called in a panic. The government had finally made good on its threats. His room had been broken into—he said the security services had come at night. All his information had been stolen. Fortunately, he had been away.

I went to his hotel at once.

He was standing at the scene, breathing heavily, and alert. His figure and his muscles were taut, and his eyes darted between the hotel staff, me and his belongings. Unlike Gibson, this man seemed to want revenge; the government's attack seemed to arouse his anger.

The door to his room had a hole in it, punched through the wood next to the handle. The bed had been raised against a table and the mattress lifted. His laptop had not been taken, but he said that it had been hacked into—the hard-drive password had been reset—and all its contents copied.

The hotel was asking him to pay for a new door.

Just days earlier he had published a story about the president firing a senior official. The official had posed with the president for a photo on a foreign state visit, and this photo, with her image, was then printed the next day in several newspapers. The president was furious. He was sensitive about subordinates acting important. Roger had found a source in a high-ranking military meeting at which the president had vented his anger, and warned his staff never to become so pretentious as to be photographed with him, as this woman had. "In our families no one should think they are heroes." He was the sole hero.

The story also revealed something more important but subtle. The genocide had been triggered in 1994 by the assassination of the previous president, whose plane had been shot down. Kagame had always denied attacking his enemy's plane—he was responsible for ending the genocide, not for sparking it. Yet when the woman in the photograph had recently been arrested in Europe for being involved in the shooting (she was released after intense diplomatic pressure), she had not expressed frustration with the Europeans for wrongly accusing her. She had started to behave as if the president owed her a favor. "Did I shoot the plane to be jailed?" she had asked the president months before the photo incident—and the president had narrated this at the private meeting. But he had not fired her then.

Roger said the security services had come after him for reporting this military meeting, which reached deep within the government to sources that had access to the president himself. I was impressed.

But Roger was worried about something else. In the raid on his room he had lost sensitive information that he had been collecting.

Roger had discovered that the president had set off a campaign to transform the country that was not being reported in the press. There had been an order to remain silent about what was happening.

The president had taken control of the narrative in public spaces. His power was now absolute.

Roger wanted to reveal this program.

It was necessary, he said, rapping on his broken door, that the people be able to discuss the actions of the government, and that the state not be able to act as it pleased, completely unchecked. Given the tragic history of this country this was doubly vital.

Even if the state thought it was doing good, Roger insisted, that was perhaps the most dangerous kind of policy, and where the journalist was most necessary.

I felt it also made sense that Roger leave the capital, for his safety.

He agreed, and suggested that he take me along so we could verify what was happening. Roger had various leads; there was apparently a place where officials had filled an entire school with people; it evoked scenes from the genocide.

His only concern was whether we should travel together. A foreigner would attract attention. I told Roger I wanted to see the president's program.

He said we would go south.

I hauled plastic covers over the computers the journalists had used in our classroom, to protect the machines from the dust. I pulled out the plugs from the wall sockets, as a precaution against sudden surges of current. Moses was preoccupied, trying to dodge the security services and treating his leg. We were going to suspend the program. I pulled curtains over all the windows, and shut the office doors, leaving the rooms in darkness, pulling all the latches firmly and securing them with heavy brass locks. I felt the pain of a last haven for journalists in the country closing to them. This had at least been a place where they could come and talk. I looked in the classroom one last time, the long hall, the whiteboard, a few handouts that I had written up and printed stacked on the table, some scribbles of the students in the room's corners, on the floor. I imagined their faces around the table. I drew the last curtain.

RESISTANCE

We were beginning to penetrate the repression that was growing after the election; we were going into it.

The people had complied with the president's order, electing him en masse. The press was destroyed. Dissent had been crushed. The people lived in fear and spoke only in praise of the leader. If there was any scent of criticism it came anonymously, as a rumor. If you were talking to someone and they gave you their name—or if you were foolish enough to request their name—you had lost that person, you knew immediately that they would only repeat government propaganda. The same if you took notes in their presence, or if you recorded their voice. It was too risky to disobey, to have any record of it. And the president, growing more arrogant in this power against his critics, had started to say more and more in interviews and on foreign television appearances—"Why do you criticize us from abroad? Why are you insulting our people by saying they are not free? Why don't you come here and talk to our people, and listen to what they will tell you?"

He said that anyone who criticized the presidential election was insulting the five million citizens who had voted for him, and therefore taking away the dignity of Africans.

It was more than anything a demonstration of his force, a force that he was acutely aware of.

The president said he had looked into the eyes of Rwandans

and asked if they were happy. He proclaimed, "They feel we are making good progress together."

He had declared the government's position, and these were the words the people knew they must repeat.

And moving within this silent country, oppressed, of words without sense—dissent banished, praise had become meaningless—I felt as if I were moving within a kind of blackness, that everything around us had not been seen, was somehow trapped where it was, that information could not escape.

It made a strange sensation: a feeling that everything I was seeing could be new. The hawk, the tree, the grass on the earth, it could all astonish. I scanned the landscape for signs of change, knowing well that the people could not speak. The idea that if something massive was happening I would have heard about it was lost. I had heard nothing; the country was isolated. Everything was suddenly possible in this place.

I felt I was traveling in a sort of medieval land, many centuries ago—it was perhaps how travelers had felt, that what they set their eyes on had not been seen by any of their people, and was independent of the world.

The farther I traveled from the capital the greater the possibilities seemed. I was waiting for something large to appear.

These were the feelings as I moved deeper within the oppression that had enveloped the country after the election.

We traveled first by bus to a main city, and from there took a pair of motorcycle taxis to the villages. But already on the way Roger pointed at the hills that we sped past, and shouted out—"Have you noticed? There are no huts."

I remembered Gibson. He had showed me that I had to look at Rwanda for what was missing. It was always the more difficult for the traveler. And Roger's comment created in me a peculiar mood—I wondered about the huts. What did their absence signify? What had been happening here?

So it began with this small sign, this remark by Roger.

More alert, I watched the people more closely. I saw schoolchildren pick out the seeds from sunflowers to eat, so that the flowers, upright, had centers that were half black and half white. Two men with sticks drove five goats along the sides of the road. And over the hills were no huts, just stretches of bush. Every detail seemed alive in the eye and in meaning, signs that something could be happening, unspoken. Roger guided the motorcycles ahead; we turned off the paved road and onto dirt tracks, climbing up the slopes.

Around us was a landscape of hills, one dome upon the other, like eggs cluttered over the earth. We became enclosed and released by these successive mounds falling away, giving us a view and rising to take away the view.

Our motorcycles made circling routes along the dips and swells.

I began to feel apprehensive. We had witnessed the growth of the government's power, and we were going against this power by coming to this area, if Roger was correct that something happening here was being suppressed. Roger seemed tense as well: he had said a few times already that we should be careful for someone might notice us.

We had not informed the authorities. It was required that they know about our presence: normally we had to explain to them our reason for being in that area and the purpose of our work. Private conversations between visitors and people were implicitly forbidden. Discussions had to be reported. Information from the countryside, even in normal times, was carefully contained. Sometimes the authorities dispatched a local officer to accompany you on your tour. It was as much to keep an eye on you as on the people you were talking to, and make sure they uttered only officially sanctioned words. I had followed these rules on my small journeys, aware of what I would receive from the people—I had then been seeking to get a sense of the government's force. But here we were attempting to move past the authorities, and directly penetrate.

Roger said this was the only way we had a hope of getting at the truth.

We rounded a curve, passed a school where we left the motor-cycles and hiked up a hill; and here we came upon a scene of sudden destruction.

Both of us walked closer to a sprawl of mud huts. It was quiet; the village seemed deserted. The huts had no roofs. Their circular mud bases stood empty-headed, open to the sky. The huts were old, their mud scarred and cracking. In some areas one could see where a hut had once stood: there was a circular trace on the ground.

It seemed like a scene of a tribal war, in which the grass roofs had been burnt off and the huts destroyed. But who would make war here?

And across from us, on the other hills, one could see the same had happened to other large settlements—a series of pillages seemed to have occurred in the area.

Someone emerged from one of the roofless huts. Roger froze. Was it a local official? They could be most dangerous, most loyal to the government. No, because he suddenly darted behind his wall, avoiding us. We followed him—his family was sitting in a circle, in silence.

Roger asked what had happened here.

But they would not tell us.

There was no sign of aggression on their bodies, no wounds. There seemed to have been no violence despite the scale of the destruction.

The earth was moist. There was no indication of scorching on it. Nor of truck tires, tractors or heavy equipment that might have been used against the people.

It was mysterious.

We walked on, and saw bunches of grass thatch lying over the ground, still tied up, as they would have been on the traditional Rwandan roofs.

So the roofs could be rebuilt. The grass was there. But the people were merely sitting, without working, without acting to alleviate their own suffering, to fix their homes.

It did not make any sense.

We passed to another destroyed hut, and from here, below us on the hill, we spotted a house—made of cement. We walked down to it. A family was inside and seemed surprised to see us. They received us. In a small room, we saw beds against the walls, and people in the dark stuffed in with two goats and a pig.

The family had given shelter to two households that no longer had huts, and had put them with the animals for lack of space.

They stared at us vacantly.

We heard a child heave. Lying on a straw bed among the animals, the child was sweating, and over his face had broken out blisters, jagged little lumps.

The owner of the cement house, a man dressed in a long dirty shirt, trousers and broken shoes, told us that the boy had caught malaria from sleeping in the open. It was the rainy season. Other children had caught a cold, something like pneumonia.

It was very difficult to care for them in his house. And there were too many in the village, all having the same problems.

The owner called on one of the families in their rooms.

Roger asked the man who appeared what had happened to

his hut—who had taken off the roof? Had it been the army? Or the local security forces?

The answer was one we would never have expected.

"We did," the man said.

Roger turned to look at me.

The man said the local authorities had come to the village and told the people to destroy their roofs. It was an order.

"And you obeyed?" I said.

"At once." He was grim, as though this should not be questioned.

Had the authorities explained their order?

"They had said the president had felt the grass roofs were too primitive."

And what did this man think?

"They are too primitive," he said. "Our country is modern now."

He said he had built the grass-roofed hut by himself, for his family, and they had lived in it for twenty years.

So what did he feel when destroying it?

"I felt the hut was bad."

A violence must have operated—in his mind—to become so convinced about a house he had made to shelter his family. That the president could say one day that it was primitive, and for him to agree to the extent that he would even destroy it. What did he think about his hard work now? That it was bad?

He said the order had come without warning, but within hours he had evacuated his family and torn out the roof. There seemed some pride in how he related this—he had obeyed the government without questioning.

He had not asked the authorities where his family would move once he had destroyed his roof. And the government had not given him instructions.

The man began to follow us, as we walked down to another

hut. Over the hole at its top, where there had once been a roof, were draped some leaves.

An old woman was lying on a straw bed inside. The bed was wet. She shivered from time to time, but otherwise hardly moved. She had also contracted malaria, we were told. It was an epidemic in the region. All the children had it now, and many of the elderly, since the roofs had come off.

The man said he had destroyed her roof. The woman had been too weak to do it when the orders came, and had implored him to help her; she had been frightened that she would not be able to obey.

The man said the whole village had destroyed their own roofs within hours of the government order.

He showed me a covered cane basket with some beans saved up from the last harvest, with which they were feeding the old woman.

The woman turned upon hearing us, and stared at us for some time. I expected an appeal of some sort for charity. But instead she started to say, in a hoarse voice, that the president was a visionary for destroying these roofs, and that this was a sign of progress coming to Rwanda. She said the president was a kind man for thinking of the poor.

It must have required a humiliation of some sort to say those words.

There was, in the middle of the village, a wooden frame—a skeleton of what looked like a home, without walls, just wooden spokes pointing to the sky. It had been abandoned.

Roger and I left the village.

We began to hike across the hills, and walk deep within the valley—some distance now from our motorcycles. This increased our risk, but we were now in a dazed state, and something drew us in. We walked through the landscape of destroyed huts, of people hiding among the trees and squeezed into neighbors' homes with small herds of livestock.

There were hundreds of people in groups of a few dozen each, under the trees and in makeshift shelters. The destruction did not end. The farther from the main road we walked the more the ruins grew intense. It seemed we could walk until the end of the land and there would only be this. And all the people said the same thing—that they had done it to themselves. That the government had told them to.

More and more I felt dismayed. The scenes of desolation, in the quiet, with the wind rustling through the hills, became heavy, difficult to bear.

The scenes were like those I had seen in refugee camps. But this catastrophe was man-made, by those the people were supposed to trust.

Roger was again concerned that someone would see us. He kept asking me what we would say. We decided that I would pose as a friend visiting him from America. But we did not know what alibi we could create for him, a citizen. There was none.

I felt we were walking too far away. The real risk was if it grew dark and we had to spend the night in this place, or nearby. Then we would certainly be reported, and discovered, and the penalties could be severe. It had become evident now that we were not supposed to see what we were seeing. That no one should know about this.

I convinced Roger to turn around. We took a curving path, up a valley and along the slope of a hill, walking past more of the broken structures, and sometimes through fields of cassava, the dark land tilled in broken lines.

On the journey back the news on the radio was still about the president receiving awards, of the government meeting its poverty-reduction targets, and of citizens announcing that they were happy and that the government was doing good for them.

When we returned to the capital we found not a whisper about the calamity. The government housing program to eradicate thatch-roof huts was called "Bye Bye Nyakatsi." *Nyakatsi* was the word for the traditional hut. The informality of the "bye bye" belied the program's true bearing. It was the president's suggestion that these huts were primitive that had led local authorities to make the people destroy them. Officially those homeless people were living in new houses built for them by the government. And perhaps, somewhere, such houses were being made. One saw photographs of the new dwellings in brief, middle-page newspaper reports praising the eradication program. No one knew of the people's self-inflicted destruction. It was as though Roger and I had shared something completely unknown, alien to the country, something purely of our imaginations but that had coincided in both our minds.

We tried. But people laughed when we told them about the huts. They said it was impossible that no one would report such a thing when the people were free to speak, that it was impossible that the president, such a wise man, would inflict such suffering on his own people, and that it was impossible that the government was causing poverty and sickness when it was working so publicly to alleviate such ills.

Almost everyone in the capital believed this—local and foreigner. Even people who had known the country for a long time.

The shroud the government had cast over society, it was powerful and effective.

So it sometimes seemed as if the journey had happened in our dreams. One could not get confirmation in the world—one had to trust only one's senses, and one's memory of the experience. Only when Roger and I got together did we know that—because our memories coincided in every detail—we had seen what we had seen. That it was true.

I now felt at a loss in the capital. I still visited the office, opened the curtains, windows and doors, but it only made me despair to see its state.

Dust had gathered over the equipment. The emptiness was disturbing. And Moses was still in the hospital. I ran a finger over the plastic covers and drew a black smudge. We could still pay the rent, but soon even that would become uncertain. I had to start to think about possibilities for the program, its future. I missed the classes. I missed Gibson. I missed the students' vitality, the moments in which we had shared ideas. Gibson's beeps came regularly, at night, but now I felt they were somehow useless. I had given up hope.

The force was too powerful. Gibson was struggling merely to survive. I had sent him money. But what would he do with it, what difference would it now make?

There were no exits. I felt Gibson was a castaway, condemned to his atrophied state, to his poverty and fears. And that this would be his life. The talent had been wasted. His beeps at night became a kind of powerful reminder of what could have been possible, of how the journalists had battled.

Soon after this I went to a government conference about press freedom. The ministry was organizing a series of "debates" to establish how conditions for the media could be improved. It was another piece of theater for the donors and foreign diplomats: the government wanted to attract funding by showing that it was helping journalists.

There had been a recent question of money. The Rwandan government had forfeited many tens of millions of dollars from the Millennium Challenge Corporation, a semi-independent

U.S. government agency, which had judged the country not free enough, transparent enough or accountably governed enough to receive aid. It had assessed that there was no guarantee its aid money would be spent for the benefit of the people when the people could not speak and had no proper recourse to justice.

This was a sensitive time for the regime, which was keen to make sure the foreign nations that supplied nearly half of its budget every year did not reconsider their support. Western democracies were crucial to this government maintaining its power—the authorities began to worry that these important funds might slip away.

The conference began mildly, with statements on how the press should learn to be more professional. But then some older reporters, whom I recognized from my class, who had once been a force in the media but were now powerless and allowed to speak, made impassioned speeches against the repression of journalists. They castigated the officials on the podium. It was not a free press—contrary to what the government always claimed—that had led to the genocide. It was precisely because the press was not free, and was controlled by the government, that the genocide had gained such force.

"How different is our country today?" said an elderly journalist, staring at the officials. "Do people have the courage to disobey orders?"

It was impossible at this moment not to think of the huts, and the obedience I had witnessed, in relation to the genocide: another moment in the country's history when people had followed government orders and done great harm to their families, their societies and themselves. The president's commands, indeed his wishes and even his suggestions, affected each village, the *umudugudu*. A similar system of villages had transmitted orders to kill in the genocide; but the president had retained this system, made it tighter. The catastrophe of the huts was the inevitable result of a government that now controlled too much.

The Western embassy officials were as usual all lined up in the last row, watching the proceedings and taking notes, as did the government representatives.

At the conference's end I went up to some of the embassy officials and asked if they believed the government was making a sincere effort. "A farce, a farce," one of them said, knowingly. "They are not sincere about stopping the repression. They are trying to distract us from the real problems."

I told him our program, the only one left in the country that sought to transform the media, was on the verge of closing. He looked at me seriously, and said I should come speak with him.

I got his business card. He was from one of the embassies that were the country's largest donors. He had a great deal of money at his disposal.

Gibson called one day to tell me of his suffering. "Life in the countryside is miserable. We have so little money we don't eat properly. I'm unable to follow the advice I wrote in my own malnutrition article. We can't afford the vegetables." He was trying, in the meantime, to recover some of the capital that he had invested in his magazine, *New Horizons,* now defunct. It was dangerous to contact the banks, which had strong links to government, but he was so desperate he felt he had to try. Gibson discovered that the magazine had been transferred in name to his best friend from the seminary, the one who had worked with us. The best friend had also emptied the bank accounts, including of Gibson's personal money. Gibson tried repeatedly to call him, but the friend would not answer his calls.

Gibson sounded distressed when we next spoke. "He was my best friend, how can he do this to me?" I told him to forget about the money, that it was gone. I said I would try to help him in some way, and that we would work together to help rebuild his life. I felt overcome.

One day, unannounced, the best friend came to my house. He was wearing tinted glasses so I could barely make out the forms of his eyes. We sat on the balcony, facing the trees. He told me to stop helping Gibson, and that he had been to speak with the police, who were aware. He was threatening me. I asked if he would return Gibson's money. He said, "Gibson is asking me to give him his money. But is it his money or mine? I feel he is threatening me. Why don't you ask the government for justice? The police have said your name, that they have you in a file." We sat, he and I, in a tense silence, looking into my garden. And the friend, looking at me through his tinted lenses, said he would leave. He had achieved his purpose.

The attendant at my grocery store told me a grenade had gone off in the city. I headed over immediately, wanting to see the scene before the government cleaned it up.

The motorcycle ride in the dark, under the streetlights, was lonely. All the cars were on the other side of the street, traveling in the opposite direction. And our road was empty—it made the impression of moving at twice the speed toward the site of the explosion.

There was a blue gas station, and beside it a dark road. I could see the glass from a distance. A minibus had been hit. Over the black asphalt was a pool of bright red blood. Two people, injured, were crying—but the crowd was otherwise quiet. They seemed detached. I stepped into a little shop to buy water, but as I entered I found the store boy with a squeaky rubber mop, cleaning up a red pool covering his floor. The rubber got caught in tissue-like human flesh stuck to the ground. Along the street the presence of the army was heavy, but the officers seemed to be ambling around. There was something strangely complacent about everyone. One felt in the soldiers' leisured, calm movements their certainty that the enemy would be captured.

And something odd started to happen to me. Each night or so when Gibson sent me a beep, I would worry about him.

I felt he was exposed.

The government was closing its grip. "We need to make residents understand the essence of eradication," said an official. They were chilling words in a place familiar with genocide. And the authorities permitted decrepit tin-roof houses even when they hardly provided shelter, when the walls were broken and the roofs had holes. So it was in reality an idea of primitiveness that was being eliminated, and already ideocide.

A small-town pastor had been imprisoned. He had called on the peasants to stop destroying their huts until the government had built them replacements. His congregation had alerted him to the destruction in the countryside. But the government arrested him at once, accusing him of threatening state security. Any attempt to break the powerful obedience the government had cultivated—even if the people were forgetting how to think and doing themselves harm in their loyalty—was repressed.

The government meanwhile continued to announce that it was serving the people and improving their lives. The president's wife promoted a nationwide mothers' health campaign, to get women to give birth in government hospitals instead of at home, and receive modern treatments like vaccinations and regular screenings for cancer. Millions of women were to be examined by government staff.

The destruction of the huts still lived in my mind. The *pensée unique* was reaching even further. It was time to go to the embassies and obtain a lifeline for our classes. The meeting at the conference had given me some hope. We needed to make sure that the government did not build on its hut program, on the power it had accumulated, and go any further without being questioned. The idea was for journalists to serve as some small check, to recover a part of their function in society: to speak about some of what was going unsaid, and by speaking ensure that the government could not simply do as it wished and was to at least some degree held accountable by the people.

A society unable to speak was like a body that did not feel pain: one could cut off one's limb and not know it, or be told that this was progress. We needed to go from a single voice to a plurality, to counter the government in this way, merely by speaking, so that people would become aware of the existence of an alternative, aware of what was happening around them. In speaking society would struggle, and feel its own pain.

Moses was enervated when he came to the office, a slow-moving hulk of a figure bending over his cane. The pressure from the presidency to have him recruited was weighing heavy. He told me that he had not slept in several nights.

In an effort to remain relevant to the journalists, not disappear to them entirely, we had begun offering money to conduct investigative reports based on proposals they sent us, on a case-by-case basis. But the proposals were scarce; we didn't offer enough money. And without training, or much experience to fall back on, the reporters stumbled. I worried they would be arrested for basic errors.

It struck me then to ask whether the embassies might protect the journalists. I thought it would make a crucial difference. It did not seem necessary to organize sophisticated support: what we needed—all we wanted—was for a few journalists to write their reports and for nothing to happen to them, or for them to be treated according to the law. This would be a starting point.

The idea, I found out, was not unprecedented. Similar measures had succeeded in other countries—Kofi Annan had for example called the president of neighboring Congo on behalf of a journalist whose life had been threatened. In Rwanda's case foreign states provided financing for half the country's expenses: they had the means to hold the government accountable to basic standards. We would ask this of the embassies.

I elaborated over a few days—working at home, on the balcony and in the office garden, under the tree—a comprehensive last-ditch plan.

We would create a corps of journalists, vetted by the embassies. Because of the lack of training and capacity, the group would at first be small. We would begin by reporting only on issues the government approved of, like progress in development programs and prominent foreign visits. The journalists would build their skills, gain practice. Slowly they would expand coverage—to innocuous but taboo topics like questioning the allocation of resources in the national budget. And finally, they would touch at the core: the enemies of the state, the disappearances, the corruption and control of the economy by the president and his powerful associates, the destruction of the huts, the traumas of history, the rumors of the secret contraception campaign against those who opposed him, his new helicopter with gold seat belts and fittings.

Even if some of these rumors were false, the press would investigate—it was as much the lies as the repression that were dangerous to society. It mattered what people believed. And, of course, there was the possibility that far worse was happening than any of the rumors indicated.

I would ensure the embassies had files on these journalists, tracking each article they published. So that when the government one day accused them of sedition or inciting violence the embassies would be able to retaliate, be able to say that they knew the journalist in question, and that the government could not simply invent information, and start to harass them.

I didn't know if it would work.

I went to meet the embassy official who had seemed sympathetic. We sat in his office and went over the plan. The official kept nodding, as I explained what was needed. He seemed in total accord. He felt the plan might succeed.

And what surprised me was that he seemed fully conscious of the situation in the country—he knew about the repression, about the various rumors. Little that I told him—even about the contraception campaign—seemed to be a surprise. He seemed aware that something needed to be done, and that because such an effort would take time to implement, we had to start soon.

He took all my papers and put them neatly in a file. "I can't officially give you a guarantee," he said. "But be assured. Put together a team of journalists."

I told Roger to hurry over, feeling that I had succeeded in something—that our trip to the huts had spurred this idea, unearthed this possibility and made me approach the embassy official at the conference.

I accompanied Moses to the office and told him on the way. He accepted the news with equanimity. "It's good," he said, seeming thoughtful.

Roger and I sat in the office garden, under the guava tree, which had begun to fruit and was giving off a sweet aroma. The paradise flycatchers filled the tree, pecking at the red-fleshed fruit, plucking out the seeds. Occasionally a fruit fell with a thud, still firm and fresh. The birds flew to the ground, rolling the fruit around with their beaks to get at the most tender portions.

There was distinct hope now. We had concrete plans to move forward with. It would take time, but at least we had an idea of how we would act. In this moment of good feeling with Roger, this sense of closeness that had grown since our journey to the huts, I asked him a sensitive question.

I had waited some time before being able to ask him this. I felt it was the right moment.

I mentioned the word *kufaniya* to Roger—the word for the president's policy of killing his own troops during his rebellion. It was a secret closely guarded, partly because it exposed his cruelty, and because it related to the president's use of child soldiers—which several warlords had been prosecuted for but he never had.

Roger looked at me, stunned.

Gathering himself, he said, "What does it mean to you, this word?"

I told him what I had learned. But I said that it seemed incredible that the president would order a cull of his own fighters—young boys who had traveled long distances to fight with his rebellion. Could he be that ruthless, and pitilessly calculating?

Roger seemed to become cold to me.

"I can't talk about it," he said.

I told him the garden was safe.

"I have to think about what you said." His face was motionless, his eyes unblinking and his breaths sharp.

He looked about us, at the branches of the tree, at the fallen fruit, the birds. I heard a noise come from the office.

Then seeming calmer, Roger said, "Can we talk about this some other time?" His voice had become tender. The tension seemed suddenly gone.

"Of course," I replied.

Roger asked to see my notes from our day at the huts. He was writing about our journey, and he wanted to see how I had described it. I drew my notebook from my bag and gave it to him. He flipped through the pages with deep interest, exclaiming at certain words, humming as he remembered the day more fully.

I saw Moses appear in the doorway. Silently, he was looking at Roger and me. With all the curtains still drawn around him he made an enigmatic figure, like someone in an old theater. He watched us for some time, his expression grim. He took a seat on the terrace outside, as though tired. But I thought he could be listening to us, that he seemed somehow tense. I knew the old man well enough.

Roger was now speaking cheerfully, and seemed to have forgotten about the *kufaniya.*

Sometimes things come together, sometimes all at once. Gibson had not communicated in several days. Then one night I received two beeps. I looked carefully at my telephone: "2 missed calls." This had never happened.

He responded to my call. His voice was clear on the line.

I asked how he was.

"I am writing again," he said.

I panicked. "Have you lost your mind? It's too dangerous."

"I need to try something," he said.

Gibson said the reports were being read out on a small private radio station by a junior reporter. They were about local injustices in his area. He wanted to do more reporting, however. He asked if we might meet. He was afraid of traveling to the capital, and so, before hanging up, he told me to come to his village to meet him when I was able to. A part of me was frightened for the young journalist. Another part, when I was able momentarily to forget the danger of his decision, was curious, excited and even half-joyful at being able again to see my old friend.

I prepared to leave—to go to him.

Agnès, the student who had survived harassment in prison, was paraded in the papers. It made me sad. She was shown prominently on the front page. She and a colleague had been shaved to their scalps. They wore the pink tunics of prisoners, neatly tailored. Agnès was thinner. Her face still showed defiance, and anger, but in her eyes something had dulled. She had suffered, and was fatigued. Her son was effectively orphaned, as Agnès was a single mother. She was penalized with seventeen years in prison for writing, the prosecutors said, that "some Rwandans were unhappy with the country's rulers." It was alleged that her words were "meant to stir up hatred and fury against the government." Agnès was found guilty by the court of disrupting state freedom—an ironically worded charge—propagating ethnic division, genocide revisionism and insulting the president.

The government had become frivolous, extreme. A minor journalist like Agnès, an already frail woman, whose newspaper sold only a few dozen copies, hardly noticed by the population, was harpooned, made to look pitiful. The government seemed to be taking pleasure in her humiliation; it seemed to be playing, amusing itself.

A little over a year later international human rights and press freedom organizations would speak on her behalf. The charges against her did not change, nor the evidence, but her jail term was reduced without explanation. It showed the arbitrariness of justice in Rwanda. Many others, with less support, received no such clemency and still languished in prisons, their cases unknown but to their families and close relatives.

I saw a full-page spread in a newspaper about a government order to make flowers obligatory in workplaces. A citizen had been quoted: "I believe plants are a source of oxygen." Small, arbitrary and superficial rules were given such prominence. Facts were turned into beliefs in support of the government, and the government's beliefs had become facts.

The hut program also continued to be covered in the papers' middle pages. It was declared to be on the "right track," to have worked so well that the destruction was to be accelerated. A rural farmer was quoted saying that the campaign had "opened the eyes of the population," and that he felt more secure in his new home. Another was quoted saying that he found his new lifestyle, without the hut, a miraculous change. "Let me be sincere," he said, thanking the government.

From the area Roger and I had been to I had confirmation that people were still living in the open. The local authorities had visited irregularly to see their plight, but that was all. And the situation had since worsened. The same was true of the area from which the small-town pastor had been arrested. People were living in the rain, and the old and infirm were dying of illness, deprived of shelter. They all asked me for help.

But they were careful to say that it was not the president's fault. He had the right ideas. It was always his subordinates who had made the errors, and even then, only from an excess of zeal.

Meanwhile, government officials publicly announced that Rwanda's growing democracy and press freedom were evident from the visible decrease in crackdowns and signs of protest in the country.

Indeed, why kill people, when they can work for you and make you stronger.

ASSAULT

It was not as I had imagined. Gibson was trembling. He seemed in a disturbed state.

I put my hand over his.

I wanted to know how he had returned. Had the immigration officials recognized him at the border? Did people in his village know he was seen as someone against the government? I wondered if he, or both of us, had been followed to the milk bar where we were seated.

Around Gibson's lips was a white milk ring. He picked up pieces of cake with a paper napkin; he bit into these. He twitched. His face was more worn than during those idealistic days when we had worked together in the office on *New Horizons*.

The woman at the shop counter was pouring milk, through a funnel, into a yellow canister. She noticed me watching her and started. A girl in school uniform sat in the corner. She sometimes glanced at us. My eyes fell on a tall man at the end of the shop, leaning on a wall by the doorway.

We were in the northern town of Byumba. Motorcycles and people passed at a leisurely pace down the main street, beyond the lace-curtained window. Gibson's village was a few miles away. He had not wanted me to come there directly. I had heard that in this area one of the president's most powerful allies possessed a farm with hundreds of cows. It was here that the president had held one of his most spectacular election rallies.

I wanted to recruit Gibson for our new program. We now had little time to lose—the free press in the dictatorship was at its end. The silence was already causing profound harm, and working on the people. But I had decided to tell Gibson only that the embassy was interested, and what we hoped to achieve. I would present only the facts. The decision to join us would have to be his.

I explained this to him as we walked to his village on the newly paved road out of Byumba. It was well constructed, with a wide gutter to one side. The mud on the hill was restrained by metal netting. The road was clean. Gibson nodded to indicate he understood what I was proposing. But he said nothing more; and I thought he was not interested. I felt dispirited. Perhaps, I thought, we had come too late; people who had wanted to speak were too terrified of the government. We passed the high arch of a prison and its iron gate through which I could see the prisoners walking in the courtyard.

He noticed I was looking. "You know many of those people have been put there for years without a trial," Gibson said. "It is how the law works. The government sees us as guilty until we are proven innocent. And this creates in our minds a kind of confusion."

The journalist twitched.

We passed milk bars, which Gibson said had become common only after the genocide. Previously, people had asked their neighbors for milk. It was an important part of the country's culture. "Milk for us is life. Sharing milk is sharing life." Some still carried on the old practices. But the genocide had ripped apart society's trust, and now the majority of people drank in these establishments, hidden behind curtains. The milk bars, on nearly every street corner, and selling a symbol of life to people, were a proof of distrust.

Gibson showed me where a dissident had once lived. It was

an open field. The house had been razed to the ground, he said. And one saw that the sand was not sand but crushed brick, that the center of the field was black from burning, that the trees in the compound had buttressed roots, were ceremonial.

We came to a gathering near a church, and the people looked at us. Gibson became tense. What is it? I asked. He did not answer. I saw a local official—a small coterie of people followed him, and he wore a jacket with the president's party colors—making his rounds. Besides his jacket, his clothes were of poor quality. He looked our way. Gibson kept his head low, and we walked.

The journalist relaxed only when we reached the other side of the gathering, though it seemed like the regard of the people was still following us. The experience had been searing—all those people; mere glances.

A pressure from the sky grew. The clouds above seemed to cook us slowly. It was about to rain. But the relief did not come; and we trudged along the neat asphalt. Like the other people on the roadside, carrying milk, bananas and hoes, we moved off the road to make way for the cars and buses thundering past. The people seemed incongruous, like on a highway—it was as if we should not have been there, that the road was not for us.

The house was a grey rectangle at the top of a hill, black showing in its windows.

Gibson was still in an awkward position with his family—it was evident in the way he shuffled past them and into his room. I saw, here, the brown sofa set from his apartment in Kigali. Two plates of food were brought to us: baked banana, beans, greens mixed with onions. He said the family wanted to help him, and had done so when he had fled. But now they worried. Someone might lose a job; another's trees might be cut down and sold; a child might be expelled from school; a bank would insist a loan be repaid at once; a doctor would not offer treatment. There was an ominous sense that something was hanging over the family, and that it was because of Gibson.

Inside the house, his nervousness boiled over. He spoke about his former best friend who had stolen *New Horizons*. The friend had also visited this house to speak ill of Gibson. The family had realized he was working with the government. Perhaps the government had offered him the magazine.

Gibson mentioned the mass distrust of the mothers' health campaign, which was making vigorous progress. Women across the country were being directed to government hospitals. And despite their fears of how medical staff would manipulate their bodies, of what they were injected with and what medication they were asked to take, the participation rate was climbing. The women were posing in photos showing they were happy at the hospitals. Gibson told me, "If we refuse, or even ask questions, they say we are against the will of the state."

I asked him about the sofa set. Still tense, he said he hoped to see his girlfriend again.

Someone came to the house, and was ushered into our room. The family, I could hear them chatter in the living room, was upset. The man had unusually bright brown eyes. He wore spotless blue overalls. Gibson stood and with both hands shook the visitor's arm. They were not strangers. The visitor, a farmer, spoke to the journalist in a serious tone. He took his leave. It was dark outside, and we heard him pass through the plantation, though we could not see him.

Gibson seethed. "The government is becoming more violent against the people."

I asked what he been told.

"The authorities have ordered the farmers to grow beans. It is a national program—the government has taken control of the land. But the farmers know yams grow better in their soil and will fetch a higher price in the market. One of them disobeyed. The government said it would forgive him, and it let him tend to the yams. When the vegetables were almost ripe, they sent the community police to rake up his field and kill the harvest."

And through the evening he kept bringing up the yams. I imagined the roots, fully grown and still alive, spread over the earth. "He wants me to write about it," Gibson said. "His children have no food."

So Gibson had become a source of some hope for the desperate.

He lay on a mattress on the ground. I was to sleep on his bed.

"I will continue with serious journalism; I can't just watch this," he said at last.

"You don't have to do anything," I said. "I think you should start your family."

"I want to. But in the end I cannot live in this way. I have to try somehow to stand up to this government. If one dies, it should at least be for the truth. One has to feel that one's life was lived in truth." He seemed possessed, in a trance since the farmer's visit.

I now felt wary. I was unhappy with the way he had taken his decision. The little twitches I had noticed in the milk bar, when we had met, now seemed more pronounced, part of a deeper terror. I had not quite felt the extent of his trauma—of being uprooted and having to return; and now of living in fear.

We were told that his grandmother had woken. She was brought into our room. I noticed how Gibson lived like a prisoner; the family was afraid of him being seen.

But I felt some hope now, for our project. It would be stronger with Gibson. I would do everything to help him. I was aware that the family would want me to leave—it was mandatory for them to inform the authorities if a stranger stayed overnight.

But I did not want to part from Gibson. I decided I would take an early morning bus. There was much to prepare in Kigali.

The elderly woman was seated on a chair in our room. It was now night, and I felt she must hardly be able to see us. She peered, extending her head toward our faces.

For a long time she sat there, quiet, her lips in a small smile, I did not know for what. The wrinkles on her face alone reflected stray light, and gave her an eerie form.

She said, "*Mwiriwe.*"

"*Mwiriwe.*"

"You are my grandson's visitor."

"Yes, I live in Kigali."

"He is a special boy."

"I think so, as well. He is very talented."

"Don't trust anyone."

"What?"

"Can I tell you a story?" she said.

I was not sure; she seemed to have something specific to say. "What kind of story?"

"It is about a cow, a hare and a hyena. Do you like folk stories?"

"I have never heard a Rwandan folk story."

"Then listen. There was a hyena and a hare. The hare was employed by the hyena to guard his cow. But one day the hare ate the cow."

She stopped. Feeling prompted, I said, "Why did he do that?"

"Because he hated his master." She was calm, and I realized the tale was an allegory.

I nodded.

"The hare took the cow's two horns and planted them in the mud. And then he screamed for the hyena. 'Master! The cow has drowned! Do something!' The hyena came, saw the horns, and pulled at them, pulling them out of the mud. 'Oh no!' said the hare. 'You have killed the cow!' The hyena felt ashamed. He thanked the hare for having alerted him, and kept him as his loyal guard."

There was silence.

"Don't trust anyone," said the grandmother.

I know, I said. But it was difficult to live in constant paranoia.

Her voice became high-pitched. "They can hurt you." She scared me.

The old woman, and her ghostlike form in the dark, made a disturbing vision. She put her hand on Gibson's head, her fingers covering his scalp.

That night was a vivid one. I did not sleep well, always imagining that we were not safe, that someone might have been sent for us or that the family, in its frustration, might do something to the journalist.

I stayed awake, often watching him.

I went to the classroom and drew the curtains open. I did it on the basis of the diplomat's promise of support, and on Gibson's commitment. I also wanted Roger to be a part of the class. Some office staff had returned, and were cleaning the courtyard of fallen leaves. The computers needed to be dusted. The roof had given way in one place and was leaking, so it needed to be fixed.

These were the little signs of life in the office. I felt glad, and hopeful. There seemed a way to advance, even if we were stumbling at every step. Sometimes Cato, the journalist who had defected to become a propagandist for the president, would stop by and look around, curious, shaking hands with various members of the staff and acting friendly. I didn't like his presence here, but said nothing.

On the radio I heard the president give interviews. He

sounded pleased; he mocked journalists. He praised his government for the "miracle" it had achieved. He said the people were free. And at government events broadcast nationally on the radio we would hear military songs playing.

Some of the staff were discussing the suicide of a university student. The government had cut his scholarship, and in despair he had killed himself. It had gone unreported in the press.

The staff seemed weary, but tried to motivate themselves. We listened to the president speak, and continued our work.

The rooms were cleaned, and the chairs placed around the tables again. It was energizing to feel the people moving about the office, to hear their voices and footsteps. I felt our program would once again live—that we had gained another chance. Only Moses seemed slow, troubled—I imagined he was still dealing with the government harassment. I tried to ignore it. Besides, hobbling about with his cane, he still managed to prepare the material for our coming classes.

Gibson was active, seeking. I again felt the man's keen intelligence and conviction. He had begun again to try to wrest *New Horizons* from his former roommate, and said he would otherwise start a new publication. He wanted to bring to fruition his idea for the magazine. He said he was also attempting to obtain, out of personal curiosity, information on what had happened to the other journalists in the country. He spoke about compiling some kind of record. Otherwise under the force of the propaganda, he felt they might simply be forgotten.

Of course, all this work, and our ability to operate, was contingent on receiving money from the embassy.

I had also been trying to meet with Roger, to discuss the program. I wanted him to teach alongside me. But he had been unreachable. Now he called me and we agreed to meet at my house.

Gibson had in the meantime been contacted by Jean-Bosco, the student who had been beaten into a coma and who had fled when his newspaper was shut down. Jean-Bosco had been looking for a reliable source in the country, and had reached out to Gibson, remembering his prize in our class.

I felt glad that this old connection was renewed. Jean-Bosco, after fleeing Rwanda, had reached Sweden, from where he was publishing the online version of his paper, called *Umuvugizi*. It was for this website that Jean-Léonard had written on the day he had been killed.

Gibson and I began, from time to time, to have our old conversations about philosophical ideas. "You know what Hegel once said?" he asked me, as we ate prunes in the office garden. "Our final cause must be the consciousness of our freedom." With Roger and Gibson, together, I became convinced that we could achieve something. I also felt the burden of expectation—of knowing what might happen if they failed.

I worried about funding. The embassy officials, each time I called, said the money was still being approved, that we would soon have an answer. There had been an unexpected delay at headquarters. I would call Gibson to report what the officials told me; I wanted to remain close to him. It was a pleasure to be able to talk to him so easily, without pain or tension—and he would encourage me. He never failed to instill in me greater belief.

Sometimes, on my trips to meet with the embassy officials, feeling numbed by the nervousness and hope, I would drive by the president's estate, desolate but for soldiers with guns. On the tall trees in his garden dark balls covered the branches like fruit, one over the other; they were bats. Their constant chitter was unnerving.

Roger came over, and he looked around my living room, at the furniture, at the walls. Uneasy, I observed the garden, the swaying palm fronds.

I wanted to plan his course. I thought that he could show the students how to set up blogs, and we would then liaise with printing shops to turn the blogs into newspapers. The idea seemed to promise.

Roger was in a contemplative mood. He said an accountant had been found murdered in the capital—as with the other killings and disappearances no one had reported it. This man had once worked in the president's party, and was suspected of leaking information about luxury private jets that the president had bought. The accountant's fingers were found broken on his corpse. They had tried to extract information from him. "You don't break fingers otherwise," Roger said.

He pointed to my roof. "You know, they can get through this very easily." Apparently in the west of the country a supporter of General Kayumba had just been kidnapped and killed. Government men had dismantled his roof, and climbed directly into his bedroom. It made a strange image in my mind, of waking up to such people. It must have terrified him.

I went to fetch Roger some water. When I returned he was standing by the door that led to the balcony.

I thought my eyes deceived me when from the harsh light Gibson stepped into the office. He was reeling, soiled. His skull seemed dented.

He fell into one of the plastic chairs.

I went over and touched his head. There was, indeed, a slight depression. It felt too smooth, too neat, and that made the form ugly, frightening.

Gibson told us that the prison had been dank, without space, food or water. The room had been full of homeless children— one rarely saw them in the main areas of the city. It was again a case of understanding Rwanda by what was not there: prisons across the country held the poor, deemed unfit for a nation striding decisively toward a triumphant future. The police had come upon Gibson after he had left church. They had put him into a pickup truck and started to beat him. When he had asked repeatedly why this was being done to him, they told him he was going to be killed. At the prison, where he spent the night, he was not registered. No one knew he was there. He had been distraught. Until the next morning, when a policeman happened to recognize him, and asked why he had been locked up. The policeman helped him get out after registering his incarceration. Gibson had come to the office.

We did not know why Gibson had been so targeted. I wondered if it was something to do with *New Horizons.* It was clear that we now needed protection from the embassies. And we needed to get Gibson to a hospital.

These were the final efforts of the free press. Moses, who seemed fatigued, told me that if we did not succeed now the possibility to speak in Rwanda would be lost for a very long time. He said they had now to give everything.

Rwanda was becoming more and more silent, quiet and calm. It increasingly seemed a harmonious country, where people spoke and acted in unison; such a place, so completely coherent, could convince anyone of its beauty.

The driver Claude came to the office porch, shaking. It was a rainy day.

"What did you tell Roger?" he said to me.

Claude, the neighborhood taxi driver who often gave Moses a free ride home, had become a friend of sorts. I had learned from him that he had fought as a soldier for the president, and we had discussed his wartime experience. He said Roger had one day seen him in the office when he had come to pick up Moses.

"Roger?" I said. "I've told him nothing. I mean, what's wrong?" I held Claude by the shoulders to stop him shaking. I could see the sweat build on his face.

"Roger told me that I have been telling you about *kufaniya*. He said that you know too much about our country. And that I should be careful about telling you such things, or something could happen to me. He asked me, 'For whom are you doing this? Does it give you money? You are giving information so you can have luxury?'"

Claude stood, in front of me, like a man waiting to be killed at that very moment, as if he were facing his death. He started to cry. He told me, "I am worried for my children."

"But Claude, calm down. You told me nothing about *kufaniya*, don't you remember? I asked you, but you told me nothing."

"It doesn't matter. This man believes I did."

"Why are you so afraid of Roger? He's just a journalist. And you used to be in the army."

"That's why I'm afraid. I used to be in the army, and I know him."

Moses—I called—told me to meet him at the stadium.

The season of genocide remembrances was to begin for that year. The president was due at the stadium. Soldiers surrounded me. I thought it was strange that Moses had brought me to the heart of the presidential guard. The soldiers had no ordinary guns; they carried sophisticated American and Israeli rifles.

Climbing the stairs, circling the cement corridors teeming with people, Moses took me to a large doorway on the second level. We stepped in, from under the roof. The green field in front of us was floodlit. Smoke rose from urn-like shapes, as a mist, dispersing in the air so that one could not see clearly and had the impression that all was blurred.

We took seats on the cement steps with the other people, who were waiting for the president. Moses was uncomfortable.

"What is all this about?" I said.

"Roger."

I asked why Claude had been so afraid of him.

"Roger is in the secret service. Military intelligence."

I waited, but Moses didn't say more.

"You are sure about this? Why didn't you tell me before? You have known now for many months that I have been spending time with him. Why did you let me?"

"I thought he would go away. But he isn't going. And you became friends with him very quickly. Perhaps I made a mistake."

My face felt inflamed, flushed with tension.

"You have to be careful with such people. You can't treat them too roughly, you have to let it go easily. But why isn't he going away? It means he found something. What?"

"I don't know. He already knew that I helped Gibson leave the country."

"He must think that Gibson works for General Kayumba. He must have believed, because you helped Gibson, that you were working for a network that evacuated journalists in danger."

"It is true that when we first met he wanted me to evacuate him."

"He was probably sent to infiltrate this network of journalists. Have you introduced him to any of your contacts at human rights or press organizations?"

"No. But he was so opposed to the government," I said. "He even took me to see how the people were harming themselves on government orders, destroying their huts. This was serious—and he wouldn't have done it if he were working for the government."

"It's how he gains your confidence. He wanted to prove himself to you as a real reporter, getting the scoop. You were not a fool to believe him. He is trained to do this."

I shook my head, finding this all difficult to believe. Moses was giving me information too quickly. "Roger had the mind and spirit of a journalist," I said. "I think he could be genuine."

"I don't think he is."

"How do you know."

Moses paused. "I know him from the rebellion."

"And?"

"Just trust me."

"I want to know."

"Why? There are some things it is better you don't know."

"What should I do?"

"Nothing. Just let him go, quietly. It is the best way."

"Tell me what he's done."

Moses grew exasperated. "Why do you insist? What do you want to know for? This doesn't concern you. Have I hidden information from you? Have I ever told you someone is dangerous?"

"No."

"I'm saying it now. Roger is very, very dangerous."

I was silent.

Moses said, "I've seen him kill. In front of me."

"Kill whom?"

"People who had to be killed."

"During the war?"

"No, after. They were people in his own unit, who trusted him. It was a dirty job. He was used by the chain of command."

Some genocide-themed songs had begun to play in the stadium, and the people seemed to become strained. The effect of the smoke was dramatic.

"Roger was sent by the government to Israel, to be trained by Mossad for a year."

I started to feel sick. What I thought was true was no longer true; what I trusted was betraying; what I believed seemed to menace. I was losing confidence in what I was seeing; the blurred stadium before me seemed to be somehow intangible.

"He specializes in counterintelligence, infiltrating enemy camps," Moses said. "It is the most demanding section—he has been trained to kill his own people, even his friends, to prove his loyalty to the enemy. He is not just anyone. He is used for particular tasks."

I felt I had no choice. The risk was far too great. "I can only take your word," I said. I felt limp.

"You have to be very careful," Moses said. "He may have written good stories. He may even go to jail for criticizing the government. It is how he earns credibility. He might pretend to be poor so he can earn your pity. I know that he lives in secret apartments reserved for the military."

"I believed in him."

"Don't think about it."

"Why would he threaten Claude, though? Wouldn't that blow his cover?"

"Probably he believed Claude would be so afraid of him that he would not tell."

The crowd had surged. One sensed that the president would soon arrive.

I said, "I am feeling as if I've been attacked. I can't believe Roger was pretending to be a journalist, when all along he wanted to destroy the journalists. This really hurts me."

"Okay," Moses said. "We should go."

"Aren't you going to wait for the president?"

"Look around you. These are just poor villagers who have been bused here for the president. They know nothing about the genocide. Look at how the Intore are trying to excite them." There were people in shirts bearing the president's face starting to sing songs about the genocide to work up the mood. "This is also his way of exercising power."

He got up.

I reflected on how Roger had lied to me. I felt betrayed, disgust. I remembered the moment when I had been moved to help him, in the schoolyard, when he had brought up the genocide, and asked if I was going to just stand by and watch, as the world had done then.

On the way out I asked Moses where he was going. He said to the house of a fellow survivor. I almost asked if I could join him, but decided that they would want privacy. I watched the old man's figure slowly snake through the crowd that was descending on the stadium.

I regretted having let Roger into my house. That Friday the latch on our gate, without me knowing how, broke—I found it so in the morning. It meant the gate could not be shut. The guard, a middle-aged man who constantly listened to the news on his radio, said he would keep an eye on the gate all night. But I was nervous; I felt the latch might have been broken by someone on purpose.

I did not know what to make of Moses' warning. Perhaps he had made a mistake? At times I believed him. At times I did not. But that night I suddenly began to feel afraid; and once the fear, the paranoia, started to build, I could not stop it. My hands trembled, and I began suddenly dropping things.

Gibson was receiving threatening calls—many each day, telling him that he was working against the government, and citing his recent radio reports. But the police beating had made him determined, and he would hear nothing about fleeing again. "It will pass," he said. I was anxious for him.

That evening I was at my desk, in a small office room at one corner of the house. The window directly in front of me, beyond my computer, looked out onto the balcony. From there I heard a clicking noise—a metallic sound—and instinctively crouched. I sat below my table. It sounded like a trigger. I waited; again I heard it. But there was no blow, no blast. The noise seemed to come from the bushes in the garden. I could not see because the lights in my office amplified the darkness outside. I was sure, however, that I could clearly be seen.

I called the guard, and told him there might be someone in the compound. He became nervous. And I heard, from around the house, him coming slowly, sometimes flashing his torch-light into the space.

The guard found no one. I asked if he was sure. He again sounded tentative. He started to walk into the bushes and plants of the dark garden. After a while he confirmed that our premises were empty.

It rained heavily that night. I heard the thunder blast. I had recently found outside our house a sick cat, which I placed on the bed at my feet. It recoiled suddenly and stared at the window. I watched its ears prick, and turn, as if tracing a sound that traveled across us. It bared its teeth at the window and hissed. I went up, parted the curtains and looked out, but could see nothing.

Barely an hour later—it was still raining—I heard a series of heavy thuds on the roof, like footsteps. The cat leaped off the mattress and crawled under the bed. When the blows continued, and I started to hear a scraping sound on the metal above us, I knew it was them—I remembered the story Roger had told me of the man who had been kidnapped from his bed after the government had gotten in through his roof. They had chosen a rainy night so no one would hear us. The cat started to yowl softly, its noise disturbing against the clatter of the rain on metal. I got up, pulled the door slightly ajar, and watched as the animal glanced up at me and darted into the dark corridor.

I followed it and locked the corridor's bulletproof door. I also locked the second bulletproof door to my room. The noises had come closer to the edge of the ceiling: they were the sounds of walking and of things being hauled to and fro. I could, if I strained to listen, also hear talking. I knew it; they had come for me. I panicked and called the guard, telling him that people were on the roof. He too became scared, and would not go to see. I told him to call the security company for support. But in such a country only the government could come after you in this manner; and then no one could help.

It was getting to the early morning. I pried the curtains apart and could sometimes see flashes of movement above, movements of dark cloth, legs, I didn't know quite what. I pulled the curtains shut and slid along the wall in the corner of the room, and waited. There was nothing I could do. The noises continued, hard, and I wondered what was taking the men so long. Outside, I had seen the sky become slightly rose-colored.

The sounds abruptly diminished, and the steps above seemed to become tentative. I wondered if it had all been to scare me, as a threat.

The guard called, and told me to come out. I asked him if it was all right—he said there was nothing, only some bugs.

"Bugs? Are you sure?" I asked. "They could not have made such a racket."

He told me to come out. His voice seemed calm, not strained.

I unlocked both the doors, and the iron grill outside; the house was now vulnerable. I slowly made my way around the house, to the area outside my bedroom. The guard, wearing his hat, carrying his torchlight and walkie-talkie, beckoned, smiling. And when I reached him I saw a million little flies crawling on the wall and on the ground. A lamp outside my window had attracted a cloud of the insects during the rains, and a horde of hawks had descended on my roof to devour them. The birds made frightening noises, like the neighs of small horses, and they were still eating, stepping all over the roof, making thuds on its surface; and below, the insects, having shed their wings and unable to fly, were trying to burrow to safety into the garden's soil.

I sat on my balcony all morning, feeling seared by the night—and I watched as after the hawks came the crows, the birds of paradise and the sparrows, taking their turns to feast.

I felt terrorized by Roger. I needed to confront him.

The beauty was corrupt. The silence had been burst open, showing its menace. The fragility of the quietness was evident. It was possible to live here and love the calm eternally, but one would have to avoid knowing its center, avoid approaching it.

The embassy officials were still telling me to wait, though they seemed less eager to respond to my calls. How should we move forward? I wanted to find a way to pick up the pieces, and to do this I needed to know the threat, meet Roger.

And somehow I also felt ashamed of that night, and fearful of it. I did not speak of what had happened to Moses or Gibson: how would I explain that I had so feared those birds?

We were at a restaurant called High Noon. And from the beginning I worried, for I felt I could be sitting beside the government.

Roger was in his habitual dress: a T-shirt and shorts. I vacillated between my present sense of hurt, and the confidence I was used to feeling around him.

He started by giving me more news: more people tortured by the government, another killing that had passed in silence. Then he spoke about his own harassment.

The sodas on our table glinted.

I said, "Roger, we can't meet anymore."

He seemed genuinely astonished. "What are you talking about?"

"We just can't meet anymore," I said. "This will be the last time we talk."

He asked if I was abandoning him.

"I have my work, and will be mostly at home. I won't have time to meet, or travel together."

He tried to insist that the journalists needed us, that there was too much to be done in the country, that the people needed our help, and that our effort would not be wasted.

I felt pressured. "Listen Roger, I can't work with you anymore."

"So it's me? It's me?" He seemed shocked, to be repulsed. "What have they told you? Who told you about me?"

It came out on its own. "I haven't killed," I said.

He turned quiet.

I didn't know if I had done right or wrong, if I had made a mistake. But I had felt his betrayal so personally that I needed to hear him speak.

"So what am I supposed to do," he said. "Go hang myself because of my past?"

"You admit it."

"Depends on what you have heard."

"You worked for intelligence?"

He paused. "Yes, I used to, during the war."

"Where were you trained?"

He paused again. "At the academy here. I was sent for one

year to Israel, to be trained by Mossad. You want to talk about it?"

I did not ask if he was sent on missions to kill.

"I'm a journalist now," he said.

"I can't, Roger," I said, looking at him. It felt painful to say that—to think that I had seen him as a last hope for journalists in the country, for the possibility to speak about the crimes, and about what was damaging people.

He became angry. "Ah, you don't care about us. None of you really do."

The anger passed.

He spoke sweetly. "I understand you," he said. "You have to respect your values."

I felt uneasy.

Our plates arrived, and Roger thanked me for the food, as he had on so many occasions. He said, looking at me, that he had not eaten in many days. I felt he was testing me somehow, that this simple statement menaced.

Regaining my wits, I said, "Tell me, Roger, where do you live?"

He seemed startled. "You know that hotel you came to?" he quickly said. "There."

I nodded. There was no longer any doubt in my mind. I was sitting next to a man of the government. He had lied about this crucial question: Moses had told me he lived in apartments reserved for the military. I knew it was impossible Roger would stay at a hotel where his door had been broken and his computer had been hacked into. He was smarter than that; but he had faltered. It was frightening.

The government was indeed everywhere, and it had infiltrated our group. I felt I could trust nothing, no one. I felt incredibly alone.

"What you don't understand," Roger said, now turning bitter, and with no prodding from me, "is that freedom is merely an illusion."

I observed him.

"You think you are free?" He started to laugh. "You have been following what's happening in the Arab Spring?" he asked. "Those uprisings are supported by the U.S. and the West."

"That's what you feel?"

"You believe people ask for freedom like that?" he said. "I don't think so. They were happy under their governments. Now suddenly they are on the streets."

I paid for our dinner. And we walked together to the entrance of the restaurant; I was with him out of fear. I did not want to anger this man, who suddenly had so much power over me.

Roger looked at the traffic circle in front of us. "You see those spies on the road?" He casually gestured to the people milling about. "They have not killed."

He turned to me.

I called a motorcycle taxi, and Roger got on its pillion. I paid the driver, and told him to go to the neighborhood of the hotel Roger said he was staying at. I wanted to show Roger I believed him.

He smiled at me, the helmet strapped to his head. I motioned to the driver, just wanting him to leave. "Stay safe, my friend," I told him.

I felt I had failed to hold on to Gibson. Jean-Bosco, from Sweden, published a story about the police harassment of journalists. Gibson insisted he had not leaked the information, that it had to have been someone from within the police. A series of threatening calls followed. A local official told Gibson that his life was in danger. The Media High Council, a regulatory body that reported to the president's office, told Gibson it was "unhappy" with him. And an Intore journalist, whom he hardly knew, in front of several other reporters called Gibson an "enemy." The community police services—people informally employed by the government—started to taunt and threaten him in front of his house.

Gibson ultimately sold his beloved sofa set, and with it, his dream of starting a family, which he had cherished for so long. He feared that something terrible was being planned for him— the signs multiplied and grew in intensity. He again had to flee. We met and agreed to break off contact. It was too dangerous for us to talk.

We shook hands and hugged for the last time. I didn't know if Gibson managed to get out of Rwanda, and over the coming days I constantly worried about this.

And so two figures for free speech in the country were lost. I was still afraid Roger could do us harm.

The embassy officials abandoned us. They had decided to support the government—roughly one billion dollars were going each year, from taxpayers in the free world to the Rwandan government's coffers.

The embassies had decided that helping the population to speak would hamper their relations with the president. "If we mention the repression to the government it will throw us out," an official said. "And then we won't be able to help anyone in the country."

It was not the first time that the world had supported repression in Rwanda. The previous regime, whose rule had culminated in genocide, had received similar praise, money and assistance from Western countries, which turned a blind eye to its crimes.

Foreign nations, by deciding to finance the government, had become its accomplices. They were making this government powerful, omnipotent, were unequivocally aiding the repression.

Perversely, the donors also promoted Rwanda as a success. Donors needed to show results for the money they spent. The propaganda, unchallenged, became convenient proof that their aid was doing good. The donors thus became reluctant to talk about repression, and eager to talk about the progress the government was making.

Money that should have come to a program like ours was given instead to the government, which was tasked with building a free press. It was absurd.

It created something like a mirage of a country—with more roads, hospitals and institutions where people should learn to think. As the journalists were destroyed more newspapers opened. The roads were kept cleaner. More people said they supported the president. People's minds were in tatters, increasingly controlled; such a state was being financed.

Donors invested in a parliamentary radio channel, equipped the National Electoral Commission with technology, funded and trained the Media High Council, and rewrote the media law. But all these projects were entrusted to the government, and served to increase the repression.

The situation in the country was worsening daily. There was little I felt that was in the realm of possibility; the power had infiltrated our effort and left it broken; the government's assault was gaining pace.

Power was consolidated. The press had been decimated and now there was almost certainly no rebuilding it. The government—

and the world—had decided the kind of country they wanted to fashion. Those who spoke against this vision knew their fate.

On a premonition that something had happened to Gibson, I broke our rule. I called him.

I found the journalist frightened. He had fled to Uganda. But there a teenager had broken into his room, and threatened him in Kinyarwanda. The familiarity, after having fled, was haunting.

And all of a sudden on the phone Gibson started to say strange things: that his girlfriend in Rwanda had betrayed him somehow, that she had not told him that she was infected with HIV.

She was the girl with whom he had wanted to start his family. This loss, having to leave her, had lodged in his mind, was like a disaster.

He said the government had found him out in Uganda, where he had registered with the United Nations as a refugee, and saw him as an insult to the nation. For Rwanda's president was telling the world his country was at peace, and people's rights were respected. Then how could there be refugees?

The United Nations was about to enforce a pact with the government to stop humanitarian support to all Rwandan refugees. The government was using this as a method to force poor exiles to return so they could be dealt with. Gibson was terrified that this could happen to him.

He kept asking me to call someone at the United Nations in Uganda, and tell them to protect him. He feared he could be attacked at any moment on the street.

And then a Rwandan journalist critical of the Rwandan president, who had also exiled himself in the Ugandan capital and had recently criticized the president's wife, was shot dead at a bar.

Gibson seemed to become uncontrollable with fear. He tried to contact his Rwandan journalist colleagues, but none of them would take action. "It is the final step," Gibson said. "They have been instructed not to write about me. Next I will be killed, and it will pass in silence. This is the final sign." The teenage boy started to appear in odd places, to follow the journalist and say, quite calmly, that he would soon kill him.

We had set aside some money at our program in case of an emergency. It became clear now that we should spend it— we were not going to receive any supplemental funding, and would soon close.

And so we organized, with what we had, a last set of classes. Moses sent out a call for participants, and brought together the students who would have been in our program had the embassy supported us.

But they were so afraid. When I spoke about the attacks on the free press, one of them stood up and said: "How can you say that our press is in decline? We have thirty newspapers, and more are coming up. We have five hundred journalists in the official register. Are we not professional journalists? Am I not speaking freely to you?"

When I suggested the government was autocratic, and that the press was needed to hold it accountable, another student shouted back at me: "We have ten political parties. How many do they have in America or France? How many do we need to become a democracy?"

Someone said: "People are free to talk in this country."

"We have freedom in Rwanda. And it is thanks to the government."

"The president has brought us far."

I felt hurt for the journalists who had suffered. I mentioned what had happened to Gibson.

"Him? We always knew he was a bad one. He was not a real journalist. He was here to incite us."

"He should go to jail, along with all the other fake reporters."

The journalists were ravaging one another. Gibson's reputation was being sullied—people said they had never trusted him. Instead of mourning that one of them was gone, and fighting for their own rights, they had turned on themselves.

The journalists in Rwanda were now sending a message that no one should do what the other reporters had done. No one should try to oppose the government.

Those who did so were the enemy.

In my first classes the journalists had been willing, more or less, to support one another. That solidarity had been destroyed. Without people willing to work together, to associate, to share their beliefs, society itself had caved in and come under the control of the government.

One of the journalists, whom I had known before, and who had been among my critics in the class, came up to me at the end of the day and put his hand sideways over his other palm. "Everything is broken." And then he hurried away.

Moses sat down beside me after the journalists had all left. The classroom was empty, silent. He said to me, "You know, I have always had hope for our country. When the previous regime tortured me for writing against them, I was convinced that it was for a good cause. Even while I was being tortured, I thought the suffering would be worth it. I survived the genocide. I saw hope. I thought that the president would bring us to something good. I fought for him to take power. But today I know that we have lost. All that work, all that pain was for nothing."

I felt attacked, harassed, distressed. I stepped into the garden where Gibson and I had spent our afternoons—it seemed so long ago—and smelled the alcoholic sweetness of fermented guavas on the ground.

Gibson had cracked, and crumbled. He trusted no one, had rejected almost everyone he knew, and was not allowing anyone to help him.

International human rights organizations in Uganda told me he was unpredictable; they found it difficult to work with the journalist.

I called Gibson every day, several times a day, out of worry for him. I tried to find him a place to stay; tried to find friends in Uganda who could help him; and I tried to get a doctor to see him.

But he was becoming increasingly difficult. He started to bawl out strings of words, half in French and half in Kinyarwanda; the words mixed up, and one couldn't quite understand him.

I thought of the student I had gotten to know in my classroom, who had won a prize for the lucidity of his writing, and who would talk with such joy of Hegel. He was being destroyed from the inside, and I could do little. I felt helpless, angry.

"Gibson, you have to see the doctor."

"I don't want to. I can't. People are waiting to kill me."

"But the doctor will help."

"No, he has been paid by the government."

"What? No. This doctor is good, he comes through a friend, trust him."

"No! No! No! He has been paid by the government. He wants to hurt me. I won't see him."

"Gibson! Shut up! You have to see this doctor!"

"He is trying to inject me! He wants to inject me with blood cancer!"

"Gibson! You need to let us help!"

"He's trying to kill me! The government is going to get me!"

"Shut up, Gibson! Shut up! You have to let us help! Just shut up!"

And I put down the telephone. I could not take it any longer. My favorite student, whom I had cared about so much, was self-destructing. We had lost this intelligent man. The government had not needed to kill him; they had just made him useless, ruined his mind, with the paranoia, by turning on him those he loved and trusted most, so that he had become a victim of that double world he had showed me, in the lights. He had been fooled by his senses, by what he saw and felt—and it had destroyed him.

The president announced that there was a vibrant and free press in Rwanda, and the population, if asked, would repeat this. The government said that journalists mostly had commercial problems: there were not enough advertisers, printers, readers. The economic abilities of the journalists were blamed; they were not good enough businessmen. The government, in its new media laws, put forward a provision to alleviate the cost of printing newspapers. The embassies continued to send their money to the government.

An order was issued instructing everyone in the country, every villager, to maintain access to a radio so they could receive government statements.

The president said that if people did not speak it was out of their own will.

The government had won. There was silence in the country. Those voices that had resisted had been hushed, and the attainment of this peace in the country had needed the liberty and lives of several brave Rwandans.

There was a last episode. A journalist managed to sneak an article into one of the newspapers in Rwanda, calling the president a "sociopath." The piece lambasted the president in passages of pure vitriol from a frustrated reporter. It read like the work of Jean-Bosco, in Sweden, and it was not clear how the editor had published the piece, whether it was an error or he was somehow complicit.

The journalists at the newspaper panicked. They were so afraid that they put together an issue reprinting good stories about the president, admiring him, praising him, flattering him. This was presented as news. The front page was filled by an image of the president and a journalist. The headline read "Sorry." The president stood tall, his hand outstretched. The journalist, hands clasped together, bowed before him.

It was the end of freedom.

April 2009—December 2013

ISHEMA
Special Imbabazi

Twohererereze amakuru
wandika ISHEMA muri
sms kuri 7333
www.ishemaonline.com

IKINYAMAKURU GIHARANIRA KUBA ISHEMA MU RWANDA

Umwaka wa II, No 25,   29 NYAKANGA - 05 KANAMA 2011,   BP 4305 Kigali,   Tél. : (+250) 07 88 51 20 14,   info@ishemaonline.com 500 Frw

IMBABAZI

Printed with permission of Ikinyamakuru Ishema Ltd.

APPENDIX ONE

Major governments and institutions that have provided support to the government of Rwanda

GOVERNMENTS

United States of America
United Kingdom
Belgium
Germany
Netherlands
Switzerland
Sweden
Israel
People's Republic of China
Japan

MULTILATERAL INSTITUTIONS

European Union
United Nations
World Bank
African Development Bank
International Monetary Fund
Global Fund

NONPROFITS AND ACADEMIC

Clinton Foundation
Tony Blair Africa Governance Initiative
Bill & Melinda Gates Foundation
World Economic Forum
Harvard University
Partners in Health

Note: This list is not exhaustive.

APPENDIX TWO

Journalists who have faced difficulties after criticizing the government of Rwanda

NAME	INSTITUTION	DATE	REPORTED SITUATION
Manasse Mugabo	Journalist, United Nations mission in Rwanda radio	1995	"Disappeared" after criticizing the government of Rwanda. Had received repeated threats from government officials.
Edouard Mutsinzi	Journalist, *Le Messager*	1995	Left in a coma from a knife after criticizing the Rwandan government; survived with grave injuries. Had written about massacres committed by the forces of Paul Kagame.
Tatiana Mukakibibi	Producer, Radio Rwanda	1996	Arrested and imprisoned for more than a decade without trial after working for an editor who criticized the Rwandan government (André Sibomana; see p. 183). Charged with participating in the genocide; acquitted in 2007.

(continued)

(continued)

NAME	INSTITUTION	DATE	REPORTED SITUATION
Gédéon Mushimiyimana	Journalist, TV Rwanda (national television)	1996	Arrested and imprisoned for several years without trial after being accused of transmitting information to Radio France Internationale that Paul Kagame was a "terrorist." Days after his arrest he was accused of participating in the genocide.
Joseph Akimana	Journalist, *Intego*	1996	Physically assaulted by soldiers after criticizing the Rwandan government. He had reported on poor conditions at Kigali's central prison.
Joseph Ruyenzi	Journalist, Radio Rwanda	1996	Arrested and charged with participating in "secret meetings," which was subsequently changed to a charge of sexual harassment.
Albert-Baudouin Twizeyimana	Journalist, Radio Rwanda	1996	Arrested and imprisoned for more than three years, first accused of reading a statement critical of the Rwandan government on the radio, and subsequently of having participated in the genocide.

NAME	INSTITUTION	DATE	REPORTED SITUATION
Appolos Hakizimana	Editor, *Umuravumba*	1997	Shot dead on the street after criticizing the government of Rwanda. Had received repeated threats from the government. His newspaper had been seized by the government a few days earlier for publishing articles on massacres committed by forces led by Paul Kagame.
Joseph Habyarimana	Editor, *Indorerwamo*	1997	Arrested and reportedly physically abused in prison after criticizing a Rwandan government official.
André Sibomana	Director, *Kinyamateka*	1998	Died from a treatable disease after the Rwandan government prohibited him from traveling abroad to seek the necessary medical treatment. Had been a prominent critic of the Rwandan government's human rights record.
Emmanuel Munyemanzi	Producer, TV Rwanda (national television)	1998	"Disappeared" on his way home from work after a dispute with Rwandan government officials about a technical error during the recording of a political debate.
Emmanuel Rushingabigwi	Director, TV Rwanda (national television)	1998	Fired after refusing to comply with Rwandan government instructions about the content of his reporting.

(continued)

(continued)

NAME	INSTITUTION	DATE	REPORTED SITUATION
Jean-Pierre Mugabe	Editor, *La Tribune du Peuple*	1998	Forced to flee Rwanda due to threats received after alleging cronyism in the Rwandan government. His newspaper had previously been seized after he criticized government officials.
Ignace Mugabo	Journalist, *The Newsline*	1999	Forced to flee Rwanda due to threats received after alleging corruption in the Rwandan government.
Jason Muhayimana	Director, *Imboni*	2000	Forced to flee Rwanda due to threats received after publishing articles about a critic of the Rwandan government. Had written about the forced exile of the former speaker of parliament.
Jean-Claude Nkubito	Journalist, *Imboni*	2000	Forced to flee Rwanda due to threats received after reporting on a critic of the Rwandan government.
Jean Mbanda	Member of parliament	2000	Arrested and imprisoned for several years on corruption charges after publishing a letter critical of the Rwandan government.

NAME	INSTITUTION	DATE	REPORTED SITUATION
John Mugabi	Editor, *The Newsline* and *Umuseso*	2001	Forced to flee Rwanda due to threats received after criticizing the Rwandan government's illegal exploitation of minerals in neighboring Congo. Had previously been arrested after alleging corruption by a senior government official.
Shyaka Kanuma	Journalist, *Umuseso*	2001	Forced to flee Rwanda due to threats received after attempting to interview a former president, a critic of Paul Kagame. Later worked for a pro-government newspaper.
Anicet Karege	Journalist, Radio Rwanda	2001	Fled the country after being fired and persecuted for reporting on poor conditions in a government prison.
Gerald Mbanda	Editor, TV Rwanda (national television)	2001	Fired after broadcasting images that showed Paul Kagame taking off his glasses, wiping the sweat from his brow and looking for a verse in the Bible, which according to the government showed the president in "bad light." Later worked for the government.
Asuman Bisiika	Director, *Rwanda Herald*	2002	Expelled from the country after calling for the release of a former Rwandan president who had been arrested after criticizing Paul Kagame.

(continued)

(continued)

NAME	INSTITUTION	DATE	REPORTED SITUATION
Amiel Nkuliza	Editor, *Le Partisan*	2002	Forced to flee Rwanda due to threats received after publishing an interview of an opposition politician. Had been arrested in 1997 for two years without trial after criticizing the Rwandan government, and publishing photos of the crowded central prison.
Jean-Marie Hategekimana	Journalist, *Imvaho*	2002	Assassinated in Kigali. His killing was not investigated.
Laurien Ntezimana	Director, *Ubuntu*	2002	Arrested and charged with threatening state security for using a word that allegedly expressed support for a former president, a critic of Paul Kagame. The newspaper was banned.
Didace Muremangingo	Editor, *Ubuntu*	2002	Arrested and charged with threatening state security for using a word that allegedly expressed support for a former president, a critic of Paul Kagame. The newspaper was banned.
Ismael Mbonigaba	Director, *Umuseso*	2003	Forced to flee Rwanda due to threats received after criticizing Paul Kagame.
Robert Sebufirira	Managing editor, *Umuseso*	2004	Forced to flee Rwanda due to threats received after alleging corruption among high-ranking Rwandan government officials.

NAME	INSTITUTION	DATE	REPORTED SITUATION
Elly Kalisa	Deputy director, *Umuseso*	2004	Forced to flee Rwanda due to threats received after alleging corruption among high-ranking Rwandan government officials.
Tharcisse Semana	Reporter, *Umuseso*	2004	Forced to flee Rwanda due to threats received after criticizing the Rwandan government's prosecution of a former president who had been arrested after criticizing Paul Kagame.
Madjaliwa Niyonsaba	Journalist, *Umuseso*	2004	Forced into hiding and to stop reporting due to threats received after criticizing the Rwandan government. Sought asylum in the United Kingdom in 2012.
Rwango Kadafi	Journalist, *Umuseso*	2005	Forced to flee Rwanda due to threats received after criticizing the Rwandan government. Was stabbed in a knife attack.
Gilbert Rwamatwara	Journalist, Voice of America	2005	Forced to flee Rwanda due to threats received after interviewing critics of the Rwandan government.
Lucie Umukundwa	Journalist, Voice of America	2006	Forced to flee Rwanda due to threats received after citing human rights criticisms of the Rwandan government.

(continued)

(continued)

NAME	INSTITUTION	DATE	REPORTED SITUATION
Jean-Claude Mwambutsa	Journalist, BBC	2006	Threatened and accused of "treason" by government officials after citing human rights criticisms of the Rwandan government.
Eleneus Akanga	Journalist, *New Times*	2007	Forced to flee Rwanda due to threats received after criticizing the Rwandan government. Had reported on the harassment of journalists.
David Kabuye	Director, *New Times*	2007	Forced to resign after publishing reports that displeased Rwandan government officials.
Furaha Mugisha	Deputy editor, *Umuseso*	2008	Deported after criticizing the Rwandan government for not investigating the assassination of an opposition politician. His Rwandan passport was not renewed by the government.
Robert Mukombozi	Journalist, *New Times*	2008	Expelled for "unobjective reporting" after he criticized the Rwandan government and reported on opposition figures.
Bonaventure Bizumuremyi	Editor, *Umuco*	2008	Forced to flee Rwanda due to threats received after he claimed that Paul Kagame had committed human rights abuses after the genocide.

NAME	INSTITUTION	DATE	REPORTED SITUATION
Charles Kabonero	Editor, *Umuseso*	2009	Forced to flee Rwanda due to threats received after alleging corruption in the Rwandan government. Had been tried on charges of defamation.
Agnès Uwimana Nkusi	Editor, *Umurabyo*	2010	Arrested and imprisoned for several years after criticizing Paul Kagame.
Saidati Mukakibibi	Journalist, *Umurabyo*	2010	Arrested and imprisoned for several years after criticizing Paul Kagame.
Patrick Kambale	Graphic artist, *Umurabyo*	2010	Temporarily arrested on charges of defaming Paul Kagame.
Jean-Bosco Gasasira	Editor, *Umuvugizi*	2010	Forced to flee Rwanda due to threats received after criticizing the Rwandan government. Had been beaten into a coma in 2007 after raising the issue of harassment of journalists at a presidential press conference.
Didas Gasana	Editor, *Umuseso*	2010	Forced to flee Rwanda due to threats received after reporting on the harassment of Paul Kagame's political opponents ahead of the 2010 presidential election.

(continued)

(continued)

NAME	INSTITUTION	DATE	REPORTED SITUATION
Déogratias Mushayidi	Editor, *Imboni*	2010	Arrested and imprisoned after criticizing the Rwandan government; charges included terrorism. Had been forced to flee Rwanda in 2000 due to threats received after criticizing Paul Kagame.
Dominique Makeli	Journalist, Radio Rwanda	2010	Escaped attempted kidnapping while in exile in Uganda after criticizing the government of Rwanda. Had previously been arrested and imprisoned by the Rwandan government for more than a decade without trial.
Jean-Léonard Rugambage	Journalist, *Umuvugizi*	2010	Shot dead after criticizing the Rwandan government. Had linked associates of Paul Kagame to the attempted assassination of a prominent dissident in South Africa.
Richard Kayigamba	Journalist, *Umuseso*	2010	Forced to flee Rwanda due to threats received after reporting on the harassment of Paul Kagame's political opponents ahead of the 2010 presidential election.

NAME	INSTITUTION	DATE	REPORTED SITUATION
Godwin Agaba	Reporter, *Umuvugizi*	2010	Forced to flee Rwanda due to threats received after reporting on a Rwandan dissident, a critic of Paul Kagame, who had fled to South Africa.
Nelson Gatsimbazi	Editor, *Umusingi*	2011	Forced to flee Rwanda due to threats received after criticizing the Rwandan government. A senior adviser to Paul Kagame had previously accused him of working with "enemies of the state."
Jeanne d'Arc Umwana	Journalist, Voice of America	2011	Forced to flee Rwanda due to threats received after criticizing the Rwandan government. Had spoken publicly about the government's harassment of journalists.
Charles Ingabire	Editor, *Inyenyeri News*	2011	Shot dead in Uganda after alleging corruption in Paul Kagame's family and in the Rwandan government.
Norbert Niyuzurugero	Journalist, *Kigali Today*	2012	Physically assaulted by police while photographing long lines of people in the city due to a lack of buses.
Anonciata Tumusiime	Journalist, Radio Flash	2012	Physically assaulted by police and rendered unconscious as parliamentarians were watching.

(continued)

(continued)

NAME	INSTITUTION	DATE	REPORTED SITUATION
Idrissa Byiringiro	Journalist, *The Chronicles*	2012	Kidnapped after questioning the Rwandan government's claim that it was not involved in violence in neighboring Congo. Held a press conference with the police days later saying he had faked his own kidnapping as part of his research.
Valens Habiyambere	Journalist, *Kinyamateka*	2012	Forced to flee Rwanda due to threats received after criticizing the Rwandan government.
Stanley Gatera	Editor, *Umusingi*	2014	Forced to flee Rwanda due to threats received after criticizing the Rwandan government on Al Jazeera. Had been arrested and imprisoned for one year in 2012 for a "divisionist" opinion article.
Eric Udahemuka	Journalist, *Isimbi*	2014	Forced to flee Rwanda due to threats received after criticizing the Rwandan government.

Note: Some individuals have, in the past or since these incidents, held government positions. This list is not exhaustive, nor does it include NGO workers, civil society members, religious leaders, academics, politicians, military officials, teachers and others.